To Ruth for unlocking
To Stu for sharing
To Patti for encouraging
To Joel for being

ACKNOWLEDGMENTS

The author would like to thank the following people without whose input this book could not have been completed. Joy Sikora, Pete Garcia, and Larry Walton for their photographic efforts. Cover photographer Jeffrey Gross and cover stylist Karen Kihlstrom. For the use of their yellow ware collections: Dr. Stu Nichols, Dr. Bornstein, Pat Bruterri, Ralph Scannelli, Evelyn Andrito, Sheldon Silverstein and Barbara Cantor. In the area of research information, a special thanks must be extended to William Gates, East Liverpool Museum of Ceramics; Gail L. Davis, Philadelphia Museum of Art; Ellen Denker, New Jersey State Museum; Mary M. Rider, The Cincinnati Historical Society; Janet Holmes and Barbara Chisholm, Royal Ontario Museum; Kirk Nelson, Bennington Museum; A.R. Mountford, City Museum and Art Gallery, Stoke-on-Trent; Dr. D.A. Furniss, West Yorkshire; John Smith, West Midlands; Tony Thomas, The Northern Ceramic Society, England and M. Lelyn Branin. A heartfelt thanks must be given to Geoffrey Godden, noted English ceramic authority without whose knowledge and willingness to share would have made the completion of this book impossible.

Thanks must also go to Irene Duvoisin, Dot Mershrod, Caroline Franz and Flo Phillips, who were always there when needed and never asked why.

INTRODUCTION

A friend once told me that an expert is someone who is fifteen miles away from home and carries a briefcase. With that many experts around I certainly don't want to join the ranks. In writing a book on yellow ware, I quickly learned that this simple, warm, utilitarian ware was steeped in confusion, misunderstanding and almost total ignominity.

For years this ware had been pushed aside as a non-entity, overlooked in the ceramic world. Because of this atmosphere, fostered in the past and reinforced today, yellow ware remains a step-daughter in the ceramic field. This book will put an end to its ignominity and begin to show that yellow ware was a most viable force in the formation of the ceramic industry in the United States.

After gleaning bits and pieces of information from existing sources, searching through museum archives, combing city directories and census data, and corresponding with British Ceramic Masters, an understanding of the history of yellow ware begins to unfold. Through research which at this time is by no means complete, one begins to see yellow ware as a transitional ceramic form that sits between pioneer redwares and modern porcelains and white wares. Yellow ware begins to emerge as a force that began to set the United States up as one of the major producers of ceramics in the world. Although I am sure many potters remain at this time unknown and much more information must be acquired, it is a beginning.

Thanks to the old masters: Spargo, Ramsey and even Barber, knowledge of yellow ware production was not completely lost, although overlooked. From these and other sources came the clues on yellow ware; and then the search for verification ensued.

This book is intended to give yellow ware a place in American history, and to be used as a reference for the collector. Major areas of yellow ware production will be discussed with a compilation of potters known to have produced this utilitarian ware. The list is by no means complete, but will give the collector a frame of reference and a better understanding about his collection. Any information concerning potters not discussed in this book would be greatly appreciated, as the study shall continue. Yellow ware, although surfacing in the early 1800s, is still virtually in its infancy in terms of an understanding of its history and its producers.

Because of its utilitarian purpose, not much has been written about this transitional ware. What has been accumulated has for the most part been pushed aside by other pottery trends. For this reason I would like to especially thank Bill Gates, curator of the East Liverpool Museum of Ceramics, for his meticulous archives, and his endeavor to chronicle East Liverpool potters in his book, *The East Liverpool, Ohio, Pottery District.* Another thanks must go to Geoffrey Godden of England, who unlocked the doors in my search for British origins. Without such people what little is known about yellow ware would have been lost.

It is for these reasons that this book had to be compiled and written, so that yellow ware can take its place in our history as a most viable and expansive entity.

CONTENTS

CHAPTER 1

YOU COLLECT WHAT?—YELLOW WHAT?

"You collect what?"
"Yellow What?"
"Oh, it's what?"
"Oh!"

Again and again these opening lines begin a conversation concerning yellow ware, whether it be with the novice drawn to yellow ware because it evokes warm memories of Grandma's kitchen, or the advanced collector of redware whose nose goes out of joint on the mere mention of the "kitchen junk"

"Yellow what" has been something that has fallen between the cracks of ceramic history and has now been rediscovered.

Not until ten years ago did yellow ware reappear in the antique world. Even then it did so slowly, and with emphatic modesty. Those collecting did their buying with apologies; "Well it's cheap", "There's plenty around," or "It does look wonderful in the kitchen". Today these closet collectors are sitting back laughing as they watch the prices spiral, not within years but months, yet still relatively nothing is known of this enigma of the ceramic world.

The mere simplicity of yellow ware has somehow lent itself to being riddled with mass confusion. Confusion reigns as to how yellow ware was made, the type of glaze used, the form and motifs used on the wares, the difference between English and American goods, and places and potters who produced it. Added to all of this confusion and conflicting information is the fact that some 90% of all yellow ware is unmarked. To the collector, these questions coupled with misinformation and the constant use of misnomer in describing the wares, can and frequently does lead to a collection of some yellow ware, some French-glazed yellow pieces and much English yellow-glazed earthenware.

Yellow ware came to America via England in the latter half of the 1820s and was being produced *en mass* in New Jersey, Pennsylvania, Ohio, Vermont, New York, and Maryland by the 1840s and 1850s. Undaunted by the Civil War, yellow ware reached its peak of production in the 1860s and 1870s. It then lost favor to white ware and the newer technology that allowed decorative porcelains to come into being. Although yellow ware was produced well into the 1930s, for antiquity sake, the turn of the century saw the demise of this so-called utilitarian ware.

For centuries, the color yellow has been a favorite to decorate with. Dating as far back as the Sung Dynasty, the Chinese found that a yellow ground or bodied ceramic was most pleasing. By the time China began to export her wares, yellow found great favor in Germany; and when it arrived in the Staffordshire district of England it was here to stay. Wedgwood, Chelsea and the Herculaneum Pottery all produced a yellow ground ceramic.[1] The early importation of these wares to America brings to light the first and most important confusion surrounding yellow ware today, "exactly what is this stuff?"

When England first began the export of "yellow ware" to this country, it was evidenced that the Herculaneum Pottery of Liverpool had at least 8 different yellow glazes to apply to a yellow-bodied piece.[2] Herein lies the difference. The first so-called yellow ware to arrive on our shores was a form of yellow-glazed earthenware showing a tinted glaze, not the yellow ware we now associate with England. Yellow ware made in this country did not have a yellow glaze, but a clear alkaline glaze. The key to American yellow ware is clear glaze. The confusion was intensified by the advertisements that came along with the English goods. One such ad appeared in the New York Merchant in 1757 and stated the arrival of "...Crates common yellow wares both cups and saucers..."[3]

In the 1890s when Barber wrote his book on pottery and porcelain, he referred to yellow ware as "Common yellow", allowing the confusion on vernacular to continue. Although true English yellow ware was indeed similar to American, the damage had already been done. It should suffice it to say that yellow ware produced in this country, no matter what color glaze was added later for decorative purposes, was produced in its original state with a clear alkaline glaze and nothing else. Too many writers on this subject have complicated this simplistic form by insisting that a yellow-tinted glaze was used. This is a fairy tale.

The emergence of yellow ware in America was well-received, for it allowed potters and homeowners to replace the porous and fragile redware that had been in use to date, with a less porous clay. The clays used to produce redware were lower glacial clays, and were fired at a relatively low temperature of 1700 degrees fahrenheit, making it somewhat fragile. Yellow ware, however, could be fired at 2,200 degrees fahrenheit, giving the clay a stronger composition.

Unusual setting of dinner plate, cup, and individual vegetable dish. Cup displays applied handle, plate is attributed to Ohio and demonstrates a heavy and crude body.

Potters also found that once prepared for production use, the yellow ware was a most maleable clay with which to work. The process of creating this clay took four steps after it was gathered. Although time-consuming, the procedure was not difficult. The clay had to be stored, cleaned, and then restored to age. After the aging, pressure was applied to rid the clay of excess water, and then it was cut into workable pieces. From this point the clay was fired twice. The first firing allowed the clay to harden in what is called a bisque state. Then a glaze was applied and it was refired to fix a clear alkaline glaze on the body. Since the clay was plentiful along river banks, especially in New Jersey and Ohio, and the process of converting the raw clay into a maleable form was not an expensive one, yellow ware was soon being produced in great quantities and became the favorite of many housewives.

Since most yellow ware is not dated or marked, confusion abounds as to the age of certain pieces. One way to help classify a piece is to become familiar with time frames in which different styles and applications were used to enhance the ware. It is most logical to assume that as technology heightened so did the appearance of yellow ware. If we follow this assumption, then we may categorize yellow ware into four time frames.

The earliest yellow ware was plain with no decoration, no foot formations or turned lips. This plain look runs the gamut of yellow ware production through the 1900s, but by the 1860s turned lips and feet appeared. The earliest pieces naturally were hand thrown, but by the late 1830s moulds had been introduced by Henderson, and moulded ware became prevalent. Although forms were simple during this period, the product line was vast, consisting of jars, pitchers, spittoons, chamber pots, teapots, tureens, mugs, cups, custards, sauce dishes, rice dishes, bowls, cake pans, pie plates, butter crocks, jelly molds, candlesticks, soap dishes, bottles, snuff jars, toilette items and nappies.

By the 1840s, decorated yellow ware was established in the form of banded ware. The first form taken was the application of one thin slip band. This was done with a slip quill that the decorator would blow through as the piece was turned on a wheel. The earliest bands were white, but soon brown, blue, green, gray, red and black bands were applied. Once this form of decoration was used, three bands were applied and so on. Possibly by the late 1850s, but definitely in the 1860s, mocha decorations were being applied by the same procedure, but two slip quills were used at the same time to create a broader and heavier line of decoration. What is interesting to note here is that many

Nine-banded bowl unusual because of number of bands it displays. Note rolled lip and foot.

Grouping of bowls showing multitude of bandings, lips, and foot designs. Earliest bowl seen in right back displaying 3 lines. Note slip application is thick and showing wear.

Nested butter pots or jars. Note banding and foot application.
East Liverpool Museum of Ceramics Archives.

12

Lipped bowls as seen in the Croxall catalogue. East Liverpool Museum of Ceramics Archives.

of the tools used to create yellow ware decorations were yellow ware themselves.

The third time slot begins about 1850 and runs through the 1870s and takes place in the Midwest, where production of yellow ware was at its height. Here we see the advent of a coarse and heavy yellow ware put into production. Its color is predominently cream or buff, but I have also seen a rich canary yellow in this coarse ware. The fourth time slot develops in the 1860s and runs well into the twentieth century. This was the era for pressed or moulded yellow ware. From this point on yellow ware had designs in the mould forms allowing for not only vertical and horizontal lines, but also scenes and floral decorations. Much of the newer yellow ware produced in the 1920s and 1930s takes advantage of this decoration. Although these time frame references only give one a minimal differential, it is a beginning in understanding the development of this ware. Too often, sincere collectors will run amuck in their endeavor to collect yellow ware by purchasing a bowl from the thirties, and wonder once it is on their shelves at home why something now looks wrong with their collections. The look, texture and design structure of the 1930s piece will stand out like a sore thumb once displayed in a collection of earlier pieces.

Still more confusion arises with yellow ware because of the names given this so-called undistinguished ware, and the multitude of shades of yellow that have been produced. As far as the names go, yellow ware has been called queensware or creamware, although it is not, cane ware because of its rich yellow color, common ware because of its ill-regarded nature, brown ware because of a brown slip application, fireproof ware because it could be used to cook with, and finally yellow ware because the essence of the clay is yellow. Yellow ware has also been confused because of its color. Shade variations are indeed numerous, ranging from a pasty pale buff or cream to a bright, luscious yellow to a dark, almost mustard hue. Were certain shades produced during certain times, by different potters? This is an excellent question, and may in the future lead to the further ability to time slot yellow ware, but as of yet this immense venture has not been tackled. It has been believed that the darker the yellow ware was, the older it was. By a rule of thumb, this is generally true, most probably due to the imperfections and impurities in the clays and trial and error in perfecting glazes. However, this statement should not be taken as gospel, for this author has seen many early pieces that are quite light in color. For the present, it should be remembered that whatever the color, and whatever the dealer calls the piece, if it has a yellow body and a clear alkaline glaze, it is yellow ware.

Still another confusion that has made yellow ware a step-sister in the pottery world is the use of different decorations and applications on yellow ware, lending itself to name changes. Decorations such as Rockingham glazes, mocha, sponge and flint enamels are merely motifs applied to yellow ware; the base or body is unchanged; the piece is still yellow ware with decorative motifs added. By any other name, it is still yellow ware.

As briefly as possible, these decorative aids applied to yellow ware should be discussed so that the reader will no longer be confused when searching for pieces. The first and most common form of decorated yellow ware is Rockingham. By the addition of a managanese brown glaze to the basic yellow ware, a tortoise shell effect is created. This glaze was dipped on or "spattered" on a revolving piece of yellow ware, causing it to streak and run, giving the piece a molten effect. The collector should be aware that unlike other applied decorations, American Rockingham is always yellow ware. The name "Bennington" is often applied to Rockingham. However, this is a town in Vermont that produced a yellow ware with a Rockingham glaze. Bennington may be classified as a type of Rockingham, but not as a type of pottery in and of itself. The use of the word "Bennington" in place of the term "Rockingham" is often confusing to the novice collector. Most, if not all, firms producing yellow ware eventually or simultaneously produced Rockingham, and by the 1870s this ware was extremely popular.

If that's not confusing enough, we can go one step further to define another type of yellow ware. This is flint enamel. The confusion here is that flint enamel looks nothing like yellow ware, but looks almost identical to Rockingham. However, there is a significant difference. To produce a flint enamel finish, a clear glaze had to be first applied to the base yellow ware. Before the glaze was allowed to dry powdered oxides were sprinkled on to the wet glaze. The yellow ware was then refired, and the sprinkled-on oxides would then fuse and bleed into the glaze, forming a most striking flowing pattern. The reason this type of yellow ware is confused with Rockingham is because the brown glaze used for Rockingham was often used for the flint enamel because it was inexpensive. More expensive oxides such as copper and colbalt were sparingly used to produce blue and green flowing lines, instead of the brown. It should be noted that unlike Rockingham, not all base clay for flint enamel is yellow. Much flint enamel was produced from a white clay. The same is true of spatter ware. Although by no means only used as a decoration for yellow ware, oxides were again sprinkled on to form a spattered effect. This type of decoration makes yellow ware more expensive than plain yellow ware. One spattered pattern that is now becoming highly sought-after is a chicken wire spatter on yellow ware. The pattern is exactly as its name implies, a chicken wire effect all over the piece. This spatter can be found in blue, green and brown combinations, and as a collection is very handsome indeed.

Mocha is another motif that is used frequently on yellow ware, sending prices through the ceiling. The confusion here lies with the fact that not all mocha has a yellow ware base, and therefore tends to be classified as a form of pottery unto itself. Once applied to yellow ware it is known as mocha-banded yellow ware. The decoration, as discussed previously in this chapter, is merely a wide white-slip band applied to the yellow ware with a tobacco leaf, worm, cats eye or seaweed pattern applied to the slip band.

This applied pattern is called a "tea" and is made up of hops, ground iron or citric acid oxides and black printers ink. Originally the "tea" contained tobacco, turpentine and stale urine. Once applied, a chemical reaction occurs which causes the "tea" to spread like spines in all directions forming the decoration. There is still another confusion that arises with mocha, and that is the belief that most of it is English. This is a fallacy that has kept many a collector of yellow ware from buying mocha. It is true that the process originated in England and was brought to this country, but the English used this motif more readily on their pearl ware and cream ware, not extensively on their yellow ware. If anything, the majority of mocha pieces seen in America today are either American or Canadian.

Another form that yellow ware takes is decorated yellow ware: the application of tinted glazes over the clear alkaline glaze. These are the fun and unusual pieces of yellow ware that add charm to a collection. These pieces may be streaked with multi-colors or may have lustre applied to form a tree of life pattern or bird pattern. A stick sponge motif may also be applied and may be found in a bullseye pattern. The enth degree of decorated yellow ware is majolica. The origins of this colorful ware go back to Spain and Holland and then migrate to France and England. In America, majolica was produced by using heavy applications of colored or tinted glazes on a yellow ground or body. Pennsylvania was one of the first areas to produce this ware; and potters experimented extensively in Phoenixville, Pennsylvania. Many pieces collected today from this area are signed Etruscan. It is evident that the more yellow ware becomes identified, the larger the expanse of a total collection can become.

This last confusion brings about yet another bit of fright that seems to enter the heart of collectors and that is the question, "Is it English, American or Canadian?" My question is "What does it matter, as long as it is yellow ware?"

Before the disagreement begins, let me elaborate on this point. The mania for "made in America goods" took a long time coming, and is important for the safe-keeping of our heritage. But when collecting, especially collecting a good whose origin is so difficult to determine, it seems foolish to bypass pieces because of this doubt.

Recently experts have come out with definitive statements concerning the difference between English and American yellow ware. However, it was Spargo who said it best some sixty years ago when he wrote, "...it is impossible for any human being, no matter how expert, to tell with certainly whether an unmarked piece of yellow ware was made at South Amboy or elsewhere. Knowledge of the simple facts already set forth, that these potteries existed at the times indicated and made wares of the types described, may be helpful to the collector. Beyond that it is romance, not history.[4] This statement is wonderful, for it deals in reality. Some experts have led collectors to believe that English yellow ware may have a white glaze inside the piece and American pieces never have this. The idea is untrue, for the East Liverpool Museum of Ceramics has

Example of late nest of bowls exhibiting thick lip and molded design of child watering flowers. Three sizes are represented here, but known to have been made in at least 2 larger sizes.

many white-interior pieces stored in their archives with the signatures of Ohio potters. Another misleading statement is that English yellow ware will ring while American will not. This is a half-truth. At times, many fine pieces made in the United States ring. The only real differences that may be used as a rule of thumb but not as absolutes is that the English yellow ware may be finer in composition, and designs may be more distinct and more finely executed. Other than that, the rest is instinct or as Spargo said, pure romance, not history. The question must be posed again, "Why does it matter?" If the collector is a purist, then he must stick to only signed pieces from known American potters, and therefore drastically limit his collection. If the collector just enjoys yellow ware, he should collect it all, and perhaps new information will come out as the field enlarges.

This leads us to the final point in this chapter, which has halted many collectors right in their tracks. "How do I know who made this piece?" is a common cry. There is no answer, for 90% of all yellow ware was unmarked. Perhaps this aided in keeping yellow ware in the basement rather than on the shelves. We can only speculate as to why yellow ware was rarely marked. The most obvious reason for this occurance was that the yellow ware was basically used for utilitarian purposes. The second reason may be

that unlike many pottery secrets that go to the grave with their owners, yellow ware formulas, glazes and moulds were dispensed across the country by potters looking for better locations for their operations. A third reason for not marking most of these wares is one that deals with the psychology of the people and times in which the majority of yellow ware was produced.

As much as we today seek out Americana, 100 years ago "made in America" was deemed inferior. This can be seen by a article written by Jennie J. Young concerning the goods represented at the Philadelphia Centennial of 1875. Miss Young wrote, "The foreign competitor comes branded as a genius, and home critics hesitate about issuing a verdict in favor of a countryman... French art is to the Frenchman the finest and the best the world ever saw. Englishmen support English art because it is their own... American art may be good, even equal to the best, but unfortunately it is American".[5] These sentiments raged well into the 1880s and 1890s. The potters themselves may have felt this way, for many either didn't mark their goods in hopes people would assume they were English or used English markings. It wasn't until the late 1870s that the first Association of Potters was formed, with one of its goals being to make the public aware of American ceramic goods.

15

Whatever the reasons for not marking much of yellow ware, the fact remains that since so much is unmarked, the collector must deal with the situation and rejoice once a marked piece is added to a collection. While rejoicing over a marked piece it must be recognized that there are still many unknown marks in the field of yellow ware. Only time and further research will correct this situation. With more and more yellow ware being collected, more and more unidentified potters will crop up and be identified. It is in this manner that a firm yellow ware history will be established, allowing this utilitarian ceramic to take its place in history.

Once all of the confusions are digested and metabolized the collector or would-be-collector should go forth into the field and enjoy this ware while the price structure is still affordable. Collect, display, and enjoy yellow ware for its warmth and its transitional history, which matches no other. The next time someone asks "You collect what?", don't make apologies, tell them the facts and see how fast their cupboards are filled.

Yellow ware bowl overglazed with Rockingham. Interesting piece due to banding coming through Rockingham glaze. Originally a plain, banded yellow ware bowl. Seen in Ohio.

Yellow ware pitcher with mocha band and applied handle. Often referred to as a turned jug.

Early rectangular server marked "D.J. Henderson, Jersey City." The mark was used within the first 3 years of business. 1830-1833.

Two yellow ware bowls demonstrating color differences in yellow ware. Bowl on right extremely heavy and coarse, exhibiting traits of 1870s Ohio pieces. Left side piece a common banded bowl with semi-flared lip found throughout production areas.

Large flint enamel cooler found in Bennington, Vermont but attributed to East Liverpool. Note the blues and green oxides along with brown to definitely distinguish this piece from Rockingham.

Flint enamel 12-sided cuspidor attributed to Lyman, Fenton and Co., showing some impressions of the 1849 mark.

Rockingham-glazed yellow ware bowls demonstrating 2 design applications.

Example of Scroddle ware motif used with a yellow clay and marblization. Note chip shows motif runs clear through piece.

19

*Attributed to Trenton, New Jersey, this yellow ware nappy displays
a cut-sponge bull's eye design. Extremely rare.*

*Pair of matched yellow ware pitchers with applied handles.
Overglazed in blue and brown for decorative sense. Unusual to
be found in these colorful glazes.*

*Yellow ware decorated plate using splotches of cobalt blue oxides
and manganese. Unusual, one of the fun pieces of yellow ware.*

Assortment of mocha-banded pieces made in the U.S. and England. Master salt demonstrates the wormy pattern, pepper and turned jug show seaweed design on mocha bands.

Late yellow ware, after the turn of the century, displaying a cut-sponge decoration.

Novelty piggy bank in yellow ware with a green and brown sponge design applied.

Yellow ware tall pitcher with green and brown sponge decoration.

Yellow ware mixing bowl with applied chicken wire sponge design. Found in greens and browns and blues and browns.

Rockingham-glazed yellow ware teapot with applied handle and button finial.

Nest of 3 mixing bowls with green and brown applied glaze in a spatter design.

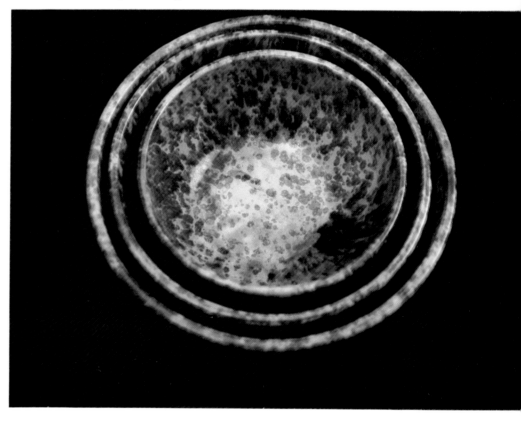

CHAPTER 2

HISTORICAL INTRODUCTION

For years writers have discussed the production of yellow ware in terms of ethereal geographical locations. It is not unlikely for a piece of yellow ware to be identified as a product of the Northeast, or "New Jersey to Ohio". Specific locations for production have seldom been pinpointed. So yellow ware has come down through the ages with no birthplace, growth place, maturation or burial ground. It surfaces from time to time as an enigma having no historical roots.

The following chapters will try to discuss chronologically by state, the establishment and production of yellow ware potteries in the United States. This will give the collector some insight on the who, what and where of yellow ware.

Beginning with yellow wares' birthplace, New Jersey, the reader will be able to view its growth, its creators and its web-like expansion from New Jersey to the north, south and west. Through this study the reader will be able to understand yellow wares' importance not as merely a utilitarian ware, but its importance in the development of a modern pottery and porcelain industry in this country. It was yellow ware which paved the way for white wares and the ensuing art pottery movement.

This section will also allow the reader to learn of the men behind the pottery—those who revolutionized the pottery industry by introducing molds and mass production; the pioneer potter and the expansionist who brought the knowledge and ability to produce ceramics back and forth across this country enlarging the pottery industry along the way. Through these historical chapters, the reader may be able to come to his own conclusions concerning the sameness of yellow ware and the reasons for marking so few pieces once he has seen the movement of many of the potters and their craftsmen from firm to firm and state to state.

Throughout these historical chapters where evident, marks used by potters will be described. Along with these marks, after Chapter seven will be an overview of the industry in the form of timelines which will allow the reader to swiftly identify times, potters, and pottery.

Histories of all things must be understood before anything came be placed in a proper prospective or enjoyed. It is no different for yellow ware. In order for it to be understood, enjoyed and cherished as part of Americana, its story must be told.

Pitcher from the American Pottery Manufacturing Co., Jersey City. 1838-1845. Demonstrates applied handles and impressed panels. New Jersey State Museum Collection, Trenton.

CHAPTER 3

NEW JERSEY

The mention of New Jersey, for some reason not quite understandable, does not send a rush through the souls of many a collector. Somehow time and "Madison Avenue" type hype has made the words "New England", "Pennsylvania", and "Virginia" send images of great antiques through the minds of collectors. Yet when one stops to look at New Jersey, the state is packed with antiquities and a history that is most fulfilling. Aside from being the birthplace of yellow ware, New Jersey can easily boast of being the mother of glass, porcelain and china in America. It is therefore hard to understand why collectors continue to ignore the status of this bountiful area.

Called "The cradle of the pottery industry in the United States",[1] the American Pottery Manufacturing Company under the superior tutelage of David Henderson was the birthplace of yellow ware and Rockingham in the United States. Born in Scotland circa 1793, Henderson arrived in Jersey City and entered into partnership in 1824 with one George Dummer, taking over the defunct Jersey Porcelain and Pottery Works. Working first with glass, then unsuccessfully with porcelain, the business failed in 1828. David Henderson then bought the company from Dummer and with his brother, J. Henderson, began to plant the seeds of modern pottery in America.

By 1830 Henderson's company appears in the "Register" of New York after receiving the American Institute of New York Award. The item read: "First Premium to D. and J. Henderson of Jersey City for specimens of superior stone, flint and cane colored earthenware, a great variety ..."[2] Unlike most yellow ware producers, Henderson marked many of his pieces. Within the first five years of business, three impressed marks were used.

1. D. J. Henderson, Jersey City
2. Henderson, Flint Stoneware Manufactory
3. Henderson's Stone and Earthenware Manufactory

In 1833 the company was incorporated as the American Pottery Manufacturing Company and remained as such until David Henderson's death in 1845. During this period two trademarks were used, neither were impressed, rather, they were imprinted under the glaze.

1. A Flag with name of the company printed inside "American Pottery Manufacturing Company, New Jersey."
2. An Elliptical design with name and address arranged around the edges of the sphere.

From 1840 until 1850 there is some discrepancy as to what happened to the firm. Spargo, in his zeal, notes that the trademark was changed once again to an impressed mark reading "American Pottery Company, Jersey City" and concludes therefore that the name of the business was changed. There is, however, no evidence of this fact, for the Jersey City Directory of 1849-50 lists the company as "The American Pottery Manufacturing Company". In 1850 the company was sold and the production of yellow ware and Rockingham ceased.

Looking back at David Henderson, he must be viewed as one the most important figures in United States ceramic history. His greatest contribution was introducing the use of moulds in the manufacturing of ceramics. This innovation immediately changed the entire complexion of the ceramic industry in America, transforming it from a cottage industry to a full-fledged manufacturing industry. "It was here that the throwing and turning of earthenware upon the English principal were first performed in America.[3]" By using moulds to manufacture goods, Henderson could mass-produce his wares and make them available to the public at lower prices than could England. It was acknowledged in an article in the *Ceramic Art* by Young, "This was also the first successful attempt to compete with England and was made in connection with the manufacture of yellow ware."[4] Henderson had begun the long drive in America to break the English importation monopoly!

Not only were his production methods to revolutionize the ceramic industry, but so were the men he brought with him from England. Henderson imported some of the greatest pottery craftsmen to help engineer the birth of yellow ware and Rockingham in America. His throwers were William and James Taylor, who would bring yellow ware to East Liverpool, Ohio and then back to Trenton to begin a dynasty. His potters were James Bennett, who would take the secrets of Henderson to East Liverpool and later to Maryland, where he would reign supreme in the production of yellow ware; and William Bloor, who would establish himself in East Liverpool then proceed to Trenton; and James Carr, who would take over the Swan Hill Pottery in South Amboy and then move to New York. But Henderson's greatest contribution in terms of craftsmen came from his modeler Daniel Greatbach, who produced the greatest hound-handle pitchers, toby mugs and presentation pieces of his time.

Close-up of hound-handle pitcher shows major differences in New Jersey and Vermont pitchers. Here the head of the hound rests on its paws. Vermont hound-handle pitchers show hound's head above paws with space between head and paws. New Jersey State Museum Collection, Trenton.

Greatbach began his work for Henderson in 1837. He distinguished himself by manufacturing an adaptation of the English hound-handle pitcher with hunt scene relief in both yellow ware and Rockingham. It should be pointed out that although Greathbach did borrow the hound-handle design from England, this design had been used over and over again throughout antiquity. Archeological digs have unearthed hound-handle pitchers in pre-Columbian civilizations as well as the lava pits of Pompeii.[5] So Greatbach's adaptation can be seen as no less than good taste. After producing his pitchers and tobys, Greatbach left Henderson and spent time working for or distributing to the Salamander Pottery, Congress Pottery and Hawkes and Taylor and Company of Ohio. It is erroneously believed by some that by 1852 Greatbach entered into partnership with James Carr of the Swan Hill Pottery in South Amboy. This partnership, unless very silent, could not have taken place at this time, for Greatbach was on his way to Vermont and the United States Pottery Company by late 1851. This fact is substanciated by the Jersey City Directory of 1851 which omits Greatbach's name. Still further proof of his Vermont move was seen at the New York Exhibition in 1853, where Greatbach's work was displayed in the booth of Mr. Fenton, owner of the United States Pottery Company.

It was in Vermont under the direction of Fenton that Greatbach really flourished. The Bennington version of the hound-handle pitcher is indeed the best produced in the nineteenth century. It is easily distinguished from the New Jersey pitcher in that the character of the piece is much sharper, especially the head. Credit, of course, must go to the New Jersey pitcher for being the first, but unlike the Bennington version, the Jersey hound resembles a serpent with a headache rather than a dog. Another distinguishing factor is that most of the Bennington pieces have the head arched above the hound's paws, while the Jersey version many times has the head touching the rim of the pitcher. Henderson and Greatbach had indeed set the stage for future potters.

The Raritan River, with healthy clay deposits surrounding her banks, soon had potteries dotting the landscape. Word of the great opportunities to produce a cheap and functional ceramic made from the maleable yellow clay spread quickly. In 1825 the Salamander Works was founded in Woodbridge, New Jersey and would continue as a viable pottery until 1891, when fire gutted the building. The production of yellow ware did not begin until 1836, when the pottery was being operated by two Frenchmen, Michael Lefoulon and Henry DeCasse.

The company produced a great amount of toby mugs and pitchers until 1850, when DeCasse left the business. Common to this firm were hound-handle pitchers with relief decoration of scrolls, ivy and fawns. Between 1835 and 1845, a Rockingham-glazed yellow ware pitcher was manufactured showing a relief design of a fire engine being pulled to a farmhouse. The neck relief was executed with green briar vines, which will help the collector to identify a New Jersey piece since these vines are native to the state. The mark found on Salamander pieces read "Salamander/ Works/ Cannon Street/ New York", which has led some to believe it was a New York firm. Actually, only the sales office and showroom were located at this address. All manufacturing took place in Woodbridge.

Famed hound-handle pitcher produced by D.J. Henderson, Jersey City. Correctly attributed to Daniel Greatbach. Note signature of company written in script around dog's collar. New Jersey State Museum Collection, Trenton.

Rare hound-handle pitcher showing peeling of glaze. Definitely a New Jersey piece, most probably a Greatbach mould signed "American/Pottery/Jersey City, N.J." in a circle.

South of Woodbridge in the town of South Amboy, two English potters named John and William Hancock established a pottery in 1828. Little is known of William, but John in 1829 sent for his family and two turners, Bernard Houston and Charles Harrison, who began to produce yellow ware.[4] Believed by Barber to have been employed by both Wedgwood and Clews while still in England, an interesting speculation arises concerning John Hancock. Pie plates decorated with pink lustre have been attributed to south Jersey, but perhaps these were Hancock's wares, since Wedgwood was a master at the art of lustre. As noted this is mere speculation, for no markings have been found to date on these lustre pieces. Some pieces from the Hancock Pottery, however, were marked "Hancock Potter".

By 1840 Hancock sold his pottery to George Price, who converted the works into a stoneware factory. Hancock at this time left the state of New Jersey and ventured to Louisville, Kentucky to set up a stoneware pottery. Not much is known of this venture except that it was short-lived. By the following year he arrived in East Liverpool, Ohio and purchased a pottery called Mansion House, formerly owned by Salt and Mear. Within the year, however, Hancock died.

Further north in Elizabeth, New Jersey, John Pruden went into partnership with his father in 1835 in the production of yellow ware and Rockingham. The factory had originally been owned by Edward Griffin, where in 1811 he began the production of stoneware. By 1820 Keen

Attributed to John Hancock due to his lustre work in England. This pie plate exhibits lustre overglaze depicting the Tree of Life pattern. Other lustre decorations can be found on yellow ware, although this is not common due to the expertise needed for lustre application.

Pruden, John's father, bought the large factory and continued to make stoneware and redware. Interestingly enough, the Pruden factory was one of the few to produce redware in New Jersey. When John took the firm over, Keen Pruden went on to become a Director of the State Bank and helped to found the Elizabethtown Water Company. His pottery remained in existence until 1879.

Newark was the site of two little-known potteries founded in the 1830s-1840s. The first was established in 1836 by Balthasar Krumeich and was located at 44 Canal Street. Here he produced both yellow ware and brown ware for kitchen use. The pottery remained owned and operated by the family until circa 1900. The second pottery in Newark was founded by Daniel Gillig in 1840. This pottery was located at Ogden and Division Streets. By 1855 Gillig took a partner by the name of Williams. This partnership was shortlived; by 1856 Williams sold his interest to John H. Osborne, who took complete control of the company in 1862. Later, his sons, John H. and John C., would carry on the works until 1900. Little is really known of this pottery other than it did produce drainpipe and firebrick. An advertisement from 1872 would have one believe that yellow ware and Rockingham were also produced, but what is more likely is that these goods were wholesaled or retailed by the firm and not produced by them.

Hound-handle pitcher produced by Abraham Cadmus of the Congress Pottery. Note the vine leaves around neck of this piece. These leaves are native to New Jersey. This pitcher is assumed to have been produced from a Greatbach mould. New Jersey State Museum Collection, Trenton.

Back in South Amboy the defunct Hancock Pottery was acquired by Abraham Cadmus, a New York businessman, in 1849. It is likely that Cadmus rebuilt the pottery and named it The Congress Pottery. It will also be seen shortly that he had a hand in the Swan Hill Pottery, next to be discussed. Cadmus ran the Congress Pottery until his death in 1854. By 1857 Joseph Wooton, who would later be seen on the payroll of the Swan Hill Pottery, took over the company, but by 1860 the company passed on to William Allen. In 1861 the building burned to the ground.

The Congress Pottery under the direction of Cadmus produced hound-handle pitchers, which were probably models made by Greatbach. One impressive piece sits in the New Jersey Museum. It is a yellow ware pitcher with a relief of a fire company pulling an engine. The mark employed by Cadmus on some pieces was "A. Cadmus/

Congress Pottery/ South Amboy/ New Jersey". Within one year, Cadmus would expand and lease the Swan Hill Pottery, changing its name for a time to the Cadmus Pottery.

Spargo states in *Early American Pottery & China* that it is "impossible to tell" which pottery, either Hancock, Cadmus or Swan Hill, produced which unmarked pieces of yellow ware, since Cadmus had a hand in each of the potteries at some time, and many of the moulds used were interchanged. The same year that Cadmus was forming the Congress Pottery, South Amboy saw the birth of the Swan Hill Pottery.

The Swan Hill Pottery had a twenty-seven year history, from 1849 to 1876, encompassing nine owners. At times its history is somewhat fuzzy as to owners and dates, however it can be pieced with some semblance of reliability. The

A LIST OF
PRICES OF EARTHENWARE, &C.

MANUFACTURED AT

SWAN HILL POTTERY, SOUTH AMBOY, N. J.

JAMES CARR, THOMAS LOCKER AND JOSEPH WOOTON, Proprietors.

WHITE WARE.

French Shape Bed Pans, No. 1 $9.00, No. 2 $8.00 per dozen.
Round " " $8.50 $7.50 "
Slop Jars, Washington shape, $2.50 each.
Urinals, each kind, $4.50 per dozen.
Coach Pans, "
Chair Pans, 5, 6, 7, 8, 9, 10, 11, 12 inches. 11, 13, 16, 20, 25, 30, 35, 40 cents each.
Round Fluted Soaps and Drainers, $1.62 $1.37½ per dozen.
Oval Bird Baths, No. 1 $1.00, No. 2 75 cts. No. 3 62½ cts. per dozen.
Thrown Flanged Mugs, 24s. 75 cts. 30s. 62½ cts. per dozen.
Mustard Pots and Covers, 62½ cts. per dozen.
Paste Boxes, ¾ to 2 oz. $6.00, 3 oz. $8.00, 4 oz. $10.50, 6 oz. $12.50 per gross.
Ointment Jars, 36s. 62½ cts. 30s. 75 cts. 24s. 87½ cts. Mass. 87½ cts. per dozen.
Jelly Cans, 36s. 30, 30s. 35, 24s. 42, 18s. 55, 12s. 80, 6s. $1.10, 4s. $1.60, 3s. $2.35, 2s. $3.10 per dozen.

YELLOW WARE.

Slop Jars, Washington shape, $1.75 each.
Grape Ice Pitchers, covered, $7.50 per dozen.
French shape Bed Pans, No. 1 $6.00, No. 2 $5.00 per dozen.
Round " " 5.75, 4.75 "
Dipt Chambers, 4s. $3.00, 6s. $2.25, 9s. $1.87½, 12s. $1.37½ per dozen.
" Pitchers, 3s. $3.50, 4s. $2.75, 6s. $2.00, 12s. $1.12, 24s. 65 cts. per dozen.
" Bowls, 3s. $3.50, 4s. $2.50, 9s. $1.87, 9s. $1.25, 12s. $1.00, 24s. 45, 30s. 38, 36s. 32 cts. per dozen.
Lipped Bowls, 3s. $4.00, 4s. $3.56, 6s. $2.70, 9s. $1.75, 12s. $1.25 per dozen.
Salts, 25 cts. Mustards, 50 cts. per dozen.
Round Pie Plates, 7, 8, 9, 10, 11 inches. 43, 53, 64, 85, $1.05 per dozen.
Round Nappies, 6, 7, 8, 9, 10, 11, 12 inches. 43, 53, 64, 74, 95, $1.25, $1.75 per dozen.
Square Pie Plates, 7, 8, 9, 10, 11, 12 inches. 64, 85, $1.05, $1.25, $1.70, $2.10 per dozen.
Cake Pans, 8, 9, 10, 11, 12 inches. 90, $1.35, $1.90, $2.55, $3.40 per dozen.

Bakers' Pans, 8, 85, 9, $1.16, 10, $1.50, 11, $2.10, 12, $2.55 per dozen.

ENAMELED ROCKINGHAM WARE.

Water Tanks, Barrel shape, No. 1 $3.50, No. 2 $2.50 each.
Bed Pans, French shape, $6.50, $5.50 per dozen.
Slop Jars, Washington shape, $2.00 per dozen.
Ewer and Basins " " $9.00 per dozen.
Chambers, cov'd, " " $5.00 per dozen.
Soaps and Drainers, Washington shape, No. 1 $1.12½, No. 2 87½ cts. per dozen.
Flanged Mugs, 24s. 62½, 30s. 50 cts. per dozen.
Tall Mugs, (Measure,) Quart. $1.00, Pint. 75, ½ Pint. 44 cts. per dozen.
Goblets, $1.50 per dozen.
Tumblers, 50 cts. per dozen.
Tobys, (Wafer Pots,) $1.50 per dozen.
Preserve Jars, 1 Gall. $3.00, ¾ Gall. $2.50, ½ Gall. $2.00, ¼ Gall. $1.75, ⅛ Gall. $1.50 per dozen.
Pressed Teapots, $3.00, $2.50 per dozen.
Thrown Teapots, 1st. $2.50, 2d. $2.00, 3d. $1.75 per dozen.
Brown Globe-footed Sugars, $1.00 per dozen.
Pipkins, 1st. $6.00, 2d. $4.50, 3d. $3.50, 4th. $2.50, 5th. $1.75 per dozen.
Covered Grape Ice Pitchers, No. 1 $8.00, No. 2 $6.50, No. 3 $2.50 per dozen.
Uncov'd " $5.00, $3.75, $1.50 per dozen.
Round Flute Pitchers, (Washington,) 1st. $4.25, 2d. $3.50, 3d. $1.50 per dozen.
French Flute Spittoons, 1st. $5.00, 2d. $4.00, 3d. $2.50, 4th. $1.25 per dozen.
Funnel Spittoons, $1.50 per dozen.
Victoria Spittoons, 1st. $5.00, 2d. $4.00, 3d. $3.00, 4th. $2.12½ per dozen.
Round Spittoons, 1st. $4.00, 2d. $2.25, 3d. $1.75 per dozen.
Oblong Spittoons, 1st. $4.00, 2d. $3.00, 3d. $2.25 per dozen.
Apostle Spittoons, 1st. $4.00, 2d. $3.00, 3d. $2.25 per dozen.
Reverse Flute Spittoons, 1st. $3.00, 2d. $2.25 per dozen.

Price list from the Swan Hill Pottery under the direction of Carr, Locker, and Wooten from 1852-55. New Jersey State Museum Collection, Trenton.

pottery was initially founded by Sparks and Moore, about whom virtually nothing is known other that their chief potter was probably Thomas Locker. Within the year the firm was sold to Charles Fish and Edward Hanks, but these gentlemen only ran the firm for a few months putting out yellow ware marked with an impressed swan with "Hanks and Fish/ Swan Hill/ Pottery/ S. Amboy, New Jersey" inside the swan. Thomas Locker is assumed to have been the potter.

Between 1850 and 1851 Abraham Cadmus leased the pottery from Fish and Hanks and continued to produce yellow ware in the form of cow pitchers, inkwells and footwarmers. No marks are known for this period, but it is believed that Thomas Locker was once again potter, and during this time Cadmus changed the name from Swan Hill to Cadmus Pottery. In May of 1852, James Carr left the American Pottery Company and joined Thomas Locker in leasing the Cadmus Pottery. Within the next five years these two men must have taken a third partner, Joseph Wooton, for a price list from the firm lists Carr, Locker and Wooton as proprietors. During this period yellow ware was produced in great quantity, including such pieces as slop jars, pitchers, bed pans, chamber pots, pitchers and bowls, salts, round and square pie plates and nappies, and cake pans.

In 1854 the pottery burnt to the ground and was immediately rebuilt by Carr. But by 1855 he left Swan Hill, crossing the river into New York City and entering into partnership with a man named Morrison. There he established the New York City Pottery.

Yellow ware with applied Rockingham glaze. Toby mug attributed to Coxon while at Swan Hill Pottery of South Amboy, c. 1845-1875. New Jersey State Museum Collection, Trenton.

Toby mug. Attributed once again to Coxon while he worked in Maryland for Bennett Brothers of Baltimore. This is a signed piece. The two similar figures demonstrate the fact that both potter and moulds circulated throughout the yellow ware districts. Unless marked as this piece is, it would be impossible to determine manufacturer.

This is where the history begins to get less clear. It is known that after Carr left for New York, Joseph Wooton took over the Swan Hill production, but he too left, to take over the Congress Pottery in 1857. From there, some writers espouse the theory that Greatbach took over Swan Hill. This theory, however, seems unlikely, because of his involvement with Fenton in Vermont. What is more likely is that by 1857, Charles Coxon took over the pottery.

Coxon, who Spargo believes was the chief modeler for the Bennett Pottery, maintained Swan Hill until 1860. He was supposedly the modeler of a stag hunting pitcher with a rustic branch handle[7] which has been attributed to South Amboy.

Pay role for the swan Hill pottery from March 26th April 23 1870

Name	$	¢
Joseph Jackson	34	88
John Dykes	47	25
Wm Anderson	47	25
Robert Dykes	34	24
Wm Ibs	44	00
John Ibs	43	70
Charles Ibs	1	50
Joseph Maloy	36	00
Thomas Burns	44	99
Wm Wooten	51	75
Daniel Ragan	21	59
John Maloy	10	65
Shannon	23	50
James Wooten	8	40
Tim Rizons	8	40
Charles Foster	12	50
Arthur McReedy	64	92
Mrs Locker	2	25
Sarah Ibs	6	00
John Beach	47	09
Thomas Baker	44	47
Mathew Brown		
Joseph Wooten	43	28
Joseph Beach	45	10
Isaac T Rue	24	55
Winters	72	50
Wm McDones	49	00
Boy	2	50
Thomas Locker	100	00
	972	26

J. L. RUE & CO.,
MANUFACTURERS OF
ROCKINGHAM AND YELLOW WARE,
SWAN HILL POTTERY,
SOUTH AMBOY, N. J.

ROCKINGHAM WARE.

PRESSED TEA POTS.
18's per doz. $3,37
24's " 3,00
30's " 2,75
36's " 2,40
42's " 2,00

CREAMS.
30's per doz. $1,10

MUGS.
24's per doz. $0,50
30's " 45
36's " 35

PRESSED SHAVING MUGS.
24's per doz. $1,80

SUGARS.
30's per doz. $2,00

BIRD BATHS.
Per dozen, - $0,55

BIRD CUPS.
Per gross, - $2,00

ROCK JUGS.
3's per doz. $5,00
4's " 4,00
6's " 3,38
9's " 2,50
12's " 1,87
24's " 1,50
30's " 1,10

TOBY MUGS.
24's per doz. $1,50
30's " 1,25

SPITTOONS.
1's per doz. $5,50
2's " 2,80
3's " 2,10
4's " 1,80
5's " 1,70

SOAPS.
Per dozen, - $0,84

TOBY FACE PITCHERS.
24's per doz. $1,10
30's " 1,00

YELLOW WARE.

ROUND PIES.
7 inch, per doz. $0,48
8 " " 60
9 " " 70
10 " " 84
11 " " 1,20

NAPPIES.
6 inch, per doz. $0,60
7 " " 70
8 " " 82
9 " " 1,00
10 " " 1,37
11 " 1,60
12 " 2,20

CAKE PANS.
8 inch, per doz. $1,10
9's " 1,65
10's " 2,30
11's " 3,30
12's " 4,40

SQUARE PIES.
7 inch, per doz. $0,80
8 " " 1,00
9 " " 1,27
10 " " 1,50
11 " " 2,00
12 " " 2,50

OVAL BAKERS.
7 inch, per doz. $0,71
8 " " 1,00
9 " " 1,20
10 " " 1,55
11 " " 2,10
12 " " 2,60

PRESSED BOWLS.
2's per doz. $6,00
3's " 4,20
4's " 3,25
6's " 2,20
9's " 1,65
12's " 1,10
24's " 50
30's " 40
36's " 33

PUDDING BOWLS.
4's per doz. $3,25
6's " 2,20
9's " 1,65
12's " 1,10
24's " 50
30's " 40
36's " 33

JELLY CANS.
4's per doz. $2,50
6's " 1,65
9's " 1,10
12's " 77
18's " 55
24's " 40
30's " 34
36's " 28

LIP BOWLS.
3's per doz. $4,50
4's " 4,00
6's " 3,00
9's " 2,00
12's " 1,50

BED PANS.
No. 1's, per doz. $6,00
" 2's, " 5,50

CHAMBERS.
4's per doz. $3,00
6's " 2,30
9's " 1,80
12's " 1,35
6's with covers, 3,25
9's " 2,50

YELLOW JUGS.
4's per doz. $3,25
6's " 2,20
12's " 1,10
24's " 70

TERMS CASH.

Payroll of Swan Hill Pottery for April 20, 1870. Note the name of Thomas Locker, one-time owner and masterpotter, still on the payroll. Also seen on this payroll is the name Rue, who would eventually own the company, and Wooten, who previously owned Swan Hill. New Jersey State Museum Collection, Trenton.

Price catalogue from Swan Hill Pottery while under the direction of J.L. Rue and Co. New Jersey State Museum Collection, Trenton.

By 1860 the company was once again sold, this time to a man named John L. Rue. This was an exceedingly productive period for Swan Hill, and lasted until 1871. During the Rue reign two marks were in evidence. The first was "Swan Hill/ Pottery/ South Amboy" and the second was an impressed rectangle inscribed "J. L. Rue Pottery Company". In 1871 there is some evidence that Rue moved his company to Matawan, New Jersey. The Swan Hill Pottery was once again sold, this time to Fish and E. O. Howell. In 1875 it was turned over to H. C. Perrine, who had been the original manager of Swan Hill when it was owned by Cadmus. Perrine in turn leased the pottery to the South Amboy Terra Cotta Company, ending the production of yellow ware and the existence of Swan Hill.

TRENTON

One of the strongest areas in New Jersey to produce porcelain and pottery was the city of Trenton. It has been called time after time the "Staffordshire of America" because many of its potters came from England, and the area produced a wealth of wares. Although known more for its porcelains and decorative wares, Trenton began its production history with yellow ware as did many pottery areas. Why Trenton? The answer is easily summed up by one of the early developers of Trenton, C. Hattersley, Esq. He wrote: "...after traveling over the states of New York, Connecticut, New Jersey, Delaware and Ohio in search of proper materials and the best place for its manufacture, I've concluded that Trenton, New Jersey was the place

HENRY SPEELER & SONS,

Manufacturers of all kinds of

PORCELAIN, QUEENSWARE,

Rockingham & Yellow Fire Proof Ware,

TRENTON, NEW JERSEY.

ALL KINDS OF DRUGGISTS' WARE MADE TO ORDER.

HENRY SPEELER.   H. A. SPEELER.   W. F. SPEELER.

Trenton Directory ad for Henry Speeler and Sons. Speeler was first seen with a pottery in East Liverpool, Ohio.

situated as it is between the two great markets, New York and Philadelphia. Healthy, and the state abounding with fine clays, and convenient for the collection of all other materials, such as coal, kaolin, flint, sand, feldspar, bone etc. by canal or railroad."[7]

It was this man Hattersley, although little-remembered in the history of pottery production, who was instrumental in bringing James Taylor, Henry Speeler and William Bloor out of Ohio and into Trenton to pioneer a pottery industry that would eventually become a dynasty. The first man to heed Hattersley's acclaimations of Trenton was James Taylor of East Liverpool, Ohio.

Taylor came to Trenton in 1853 with his associate Henry Speeler and the financial backing of William Bloor. He established the International Pottery for the production of yellow ware and Rockingham. Together, Speeler and Taylor produced a cow creamer in both yellow ware and Rockingham. However, there is no way to definitely identify this creamer with these makers, for no mark was used at this pottery.

In 1853 another pottery was established in Trenton under the direction of William Young in association with Richard Millington and John Astbury. The pottery, located on Carrol and Perry Streets, was owned by Charles Hattersley and leased to Young for the production of yellow ware and Rockingham. Here common wares were produced for kitchen use along with a book flask (pictured) made of yellow ware with a yellow applied glaze streaked with olive green. This piece is now being housed at the New Jersey State Museum. Many of Young's pieces were unsigned, but when signed, the mark used was an impressed "W. H. Young/ Trenton".[8]

Within four years, Young disassociated with Millington and Astbury and left the Hattersley building to construct his own works. By late 1857, Young had established a new pottery on Southward Street near Brunswick Avenue, and named it The Excelsior Pottery. Here he not only produced yellow ware and Rockingham, but also began to experi-

ment with white ware. Young alone may be credited with turning Trenton into a porcelain producing area for the Excelsior plant was the first pottery to produce decorated wares. In 1879 William Young Sr. died, and his son shortly sold the pottery to the Willets family, whose production of fine china is world-renowned.

Once Young established his new pottery, Millington and Astbury struck out on their own and bought the Carrol Street Pottery. At first they produced yellow ware and Rockingham, but within three years they turned to the production of white ware. The company then took on a third partner, and was known as Millington, Astbury and Poulson by 1859. From this date until 1870, pieces were marked with an impressed M.A.P. in an oval. The rest of the history of this pottery does not concern yellow ware. It is enough to know that by 1878 the firm was out of the hands of the original owners, and continued production of semi-vitreous ware under the name "Maddock and Sons".

Before leaving Trenton, two men should be mentioned, John Moses and I. W. Cory. It should be noted that in 1863

HENRY SPEELER,

MANUFACTURER OF ALL KINDS OF

PORCELAIN & QUEENSWARE,

ROCKINGHAM AND CANE-COLORED

FIRE-PROOF WARE,

TRENTON, N. J.

Advertisement for Henry Speeler out of the Trenton Directory. Note the name given yellow ware. "Cane-colored Fireproof ware".

ESTABLISHED 1853.

WILLIAM YOUNG'S SONS,

EARTHENWARE

MANUFACTURERS,

ALSO,

Porcelain Hardware Trimmings

IN ALL ITS BRANCHES,

DELAWARE AND RARITAN CANAL, ABOVE ROSE ST.

TRENTON. N. J.

An 1877 Trenton City Directory holds this advertisement for William Young's Sons Earthenware Company. Although not mentioned in the ad, the company did manufacture a line yellow ware.

*Book flask produced by William Young & Co., Trenton, c. 1852-
1859. Book flasks more commonly found in flint enamel and
Rockingham, rare when found in yellow ware. Height of this
piece is 4¾". New Jersey State Museum Collection, Trenton.*

the Glasgow Pottery was established by John Moses, who
has been noted as a major producer of yellow ware. This
author, however, finds no evidence of the production of
yellow ware by this firm. Although the pottery had two
kilns that had previously produced yellow ware, when
John Moses took over the firm there is strong evidence that
he immediately began production of white ware. Barber
has stated that Moses "...immediately commenced the
manufacture of cream-colored ware, shortly afterwards
extended the business to the production of white granite
or ironstone china."[9] Further evidence to his non-
production of yellow ware comes from a list of what Moses
did produce. "...Mr. Moses... is a large producer of white
granite and cream-colored wares, thin hotel and steamboat
china of excellent grades..."[10] Unlike Moses, I. W. Cory
appeared in Trenton in 1867 on Perry Street and produced
signed pieces of yellow ware marked "I.W. Cory/Trenton".
It would seem from the Trenton Directory of 1868-1869,
that Cory had a partner, one Mr. Lawton. Although
numerous pieces attributed to Cory are around, he had
disappeared from Trenton by 1870.

Leaving Trenton, the second half of the nineteenth
century finds potteries once again cropping up in the
middle of the State. By 1858 the Eagle Pottery had sprung
up in Perth Amboy. It was owned by W.H.P. Benton. No
marked pieces have been found to date, although the
Philadelphia Museum of Art houses a yellow ware snuff jar
presented to them by Benton's daughter. This pottery also
produced pitchers, creamers and bowls until 1865, when it
was merged with a firebrick company.

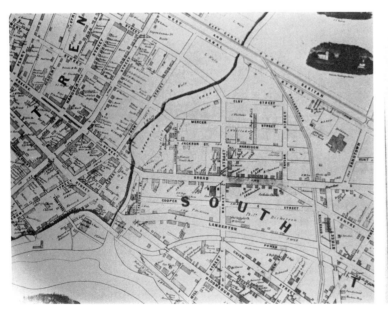

*View of Trenton from an 1849 map of the city showing pottery
district extending to south Trenton, including Mill Street, Mont-
gomery, and Perry Street.*

LAWTON & CORY,

MANUFACTURERS OF

YELLOW & ROCKINGHAM WARE,

Decorative and Bronzed Vases,

MILL STREET, TRENTON, N. J.

☞ ORDERS PROMPTLY ATTENDED TO. ☜

*Trenton Directory advertisement for Lawton & Cory, 1867-
1868. This company by 1870 had disappeared. Moulds marked
"I.W. Cory, Trenton, N.J. in existence.*

Attributed to A. Hall and Sons, Perth Amboy. A presentation piece done with a Rockingham glaze. This piece measures 8¾". New Jersey State Museum Collection, Trenton.

By 1866 yet another pottery emerged in Perth Amboy, that of Alfred Hall and Son. This pottery is, however, quite an enigma, mainly because circa 1880 there are two Alfred Halls on the books as having lived in Perth Amboy. It is the Alfred Hall who died in 1887 who is of interest, for in his will it states that he owned 461 shares of the A. Hall Terra Cotta Company. It is believed that his firm produced yellow ware, Rockingham and mineral knobs.

The last two potteries known to have produced yellow ware in New Jersey were located in Union and Elizabeth. The extent of their production, however, is not clear. The first was the Union Pottery established in 1875, owned by Haide and Ziph. This firm was located at 1st and 3rd Streets. The second company was that of L. S. Beerbauer and Company, who took over the Pruden factory in Elizabeth. It

would seem from this point on that no yellow ware was produced in the state of New Jersey past the turn of the century.

Treating yellow ware as a transitional ware, it is only natural that with the advent of white ware and the ability to decorate china that yellow ware was phased out. The industrial revolution by the 1880s was in full swing, and new and better methods of producing ceramics could only spell death for cruder forms of ceramic such as yellow ware. It must also be remembered that the mood of the people of the 1880s and 1890s was one of gaiety and almost ostentatiousness. Their desires were for the frilly and the decorative. Yellow ware was placed in attics all over New Jersey, only to be rediscovered nearly 100 years later.

CHAPTER 4

OHIO

Ohio, without a doubt, has earned the title of yellow ware capital in the United States. The areas of East Liverpool, Muskingum County, and Cincinnati combined probably produced 65% of all yellow ware manufactured in this country during the 19th and 20th centuries.

The most dominant production area in Ohio was East Liverpool, which by the end of the 19th century was dubbed "Crockery City".[1] For extensive information on East Liverpool see Gates and Ormerod, *The East Liverpool, Ohio, Pottery District: Identification of Manufacturers and Marks.* Mr. Gates is presently curator of the East Liverpool Museum of Ceramics, which contains a wonderful collection of East Liverpool wares, including a large collection of yellow ware. Also found at this museum are extensive archives which house volumes of documentation on yellow ware.

Founded in 1802, and named Fawcettstown, East Liverpool is located 40 miles northwest of Pittsburgh and 50 miles north of Wheeling, West Virginia on the Ohio River. By 1816 the name of the town was changed to Liverpool, but it remained a non-commercial entity until well into the 1830s. By 1834, with agricultural areas surrounding this waterfront town clamoring for goods and merchandise, East Liverpool began to grow. First known as a ship-building town, as East Liverpool grew, a need for utilitarian wares became evident. By 1839 the production of yellow ware had begun.[2] In 1852 the Cleveland and Pittsburgh Railroad extended their line to East Liverpool and opened the town to the world. By 1853 East Liverpool had established 11 potteries employing 387 people, and produced $175,000 worth of wares annually.[3] This was a far cry form the 1823 census, which recorded the population of East Liverpool as having 6 families and 2 bachelors.[4] By the end of the century, East Liverpool, with its ideal location on the Ohio River, plenty of raw materials, and extensive transportation routes, was the largest producer of pottery in America. By the 1860s, potters from England and the East coast of the United States set out to seek their fortunes and aid in the building of East Liverpool into one of the manufacturing strongholds in America.

From the onset of pottery production in East Liverpool in 1839 until 1872, the city produced virtually nothing but yellow ware and Rockingham. So many of these wares were produced and distributed throughout the country that they came to be known as Ohio Liverpool ware.[5]

The first potter to appear in East Liverpool was James Bennett, in 1839. Arriving in the United States from South Derbyshire, England, he started out in Jersey City, migrated to Troy, Indiana and then worked his way back to East Liverpool. Fascinated by the abundance of rich clay, Bennett founded his pottery in 1840, and by 1841 he had sent for his three brother and begun the production of yellow ware.

Short-lived in Ohio, the firm used one mark from 1841-1844. In 1844 "Bennett Brothers/Liverpool Ohio" was found on a yellow ware platter. Also attributed to Bennett is an impressed four-leaf clover figure showing no company name. Found on a yellow ware spittoon, this attribution remains speculative at this time. After establishing the pottery industry in East Liverpool, the Bennett brothers traveled to Pittsburgh and founded a pottery. By 1846, Edward Bennett left the firm to open another pottery in Baltimore, Maryland. Two years later, one of his brothers joined him in Baltimore and established the pottery firm of E. and W. Bennett.

While James Bennett was running his pottery, Benjamin Harker of England came to East Liverpool to buy a farm. He chose a 50-acre parcel of land on the Ohio River that was rich in clay and coal. Within the year he was selling clay to James Bennett and had decided to set up a small pottery on his property in a converted brewery building. Not a potter by trade, his first attempts were crude. He then leased his pottery to Edward Tunnicliff and Joseph Whetton, who failed almost immediately. By 1842 Tunnicliff had taken on two new partners: John Goodwin and Thomas Croxall. This venture, too, was short-lived, and with its demise, Harker hired John Goodwin to teach his sons the pottery trade. Left small and limping, the fortunes of the Harker Pottery took an upward turn in 1846. James Taylor, who was later to establish himself in New Jersey, joined the firm and began to produce Rockingham and perhaps yellow ware. This new partnership, known as Harker, Taylor, and Company, soon prospered. A three-story pottery works was erected and named Etruria. This partnership lasted until about 1850, when Taylor and Henry Speeler left for New Jersey. During this production period, the mark used on Rockingham was an impressed circle with a propeller figural in the center and the name "Harker Taylor & Co. East Liverpool, Ohio".

Yellow ware octagonal platter, an unusual piece marked "Bennett & Brothers, 1842". East Liverpool Museum of Ceramics Collection, Ohio.

1851 saw still another partnership formed when Ezekiel Creighton and Matthew Thompson joined Harker. These men aided with necessary financial backing, and the firm began to produce a fine line of yellow ware and Rockingham. By 1854, however, this new venture dwindled, and George S. Harker, son of Benjamin Harker, became sole owner of the Etruria Pottery. He changed the name to George S. Harker Pottery Co. While George was taking control of his father's company, his brother Benjamin Jr. established another pottery in partnership with William Smith. They began the production of Rockingham and yellow ware in the old Mansion House Pottery, but quickly turned to the manufacture of cream ware. George, however, continued to produced yellow ware and Rockingham at Etruria until his death in 1864. At that point, David Boyce, plant manager, took over the firm. The name "George S. Harker and Co." was retained, and the production of yellow ware and Rockingham was continued until 1879.

Yellow ware slip (liquid clay) applicator used at the Harker firm. This tool allowed the potter to apply the bands to yellow ware. East Liverpool Museum of Ceramics Collection, Ohio.

1853 map of East Liverpool, Ohio showing locations of early potters in the area. East Liverpool Museum of Ceramics Collection, Ohio.

Later map of East Liverpool showing increased number of potteries set up in this expansion of yellow ware production. East Liverpool Museum of Ceramics Collection, Ohio.

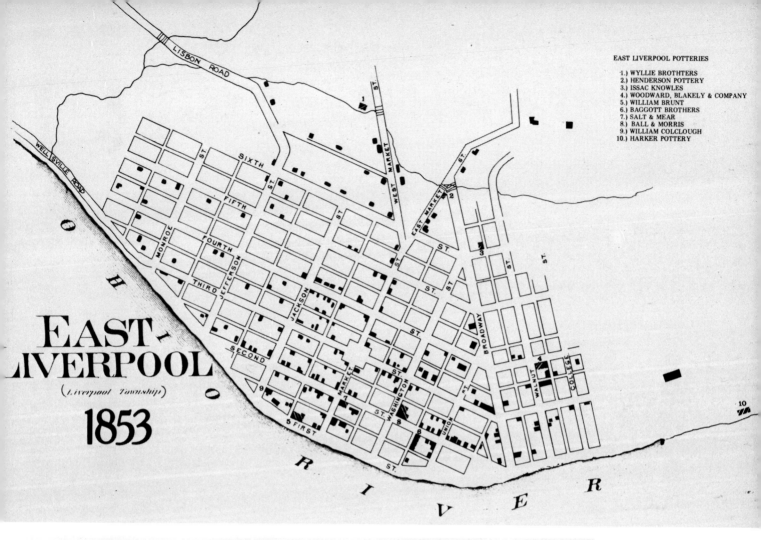

EAST LIVERPOOL POTTERIES

1.) WYLLIE BROTHTERS
2.) HENDERSON POTTERY
3.) ISSAC KNOWLES
4.) WOODWARD, BLAKELY & COMPANY
5.) WILLIAM BRUNT
6.) BAGGOTT BROTHERS
7.) SALT & MEAR
8.) BALL & MORRIS
9.) WILLIAM COLCLOUGH
10.) HARKER POTTERY

EAST-
LIVERPOOL
(Liverpool Township)
1853

EAST LIVERPOOL POTTERIES

1.) WEST, HARDWICK & COMPANY
2.) VODREY & BROTHERS
3.) MORLEY, GODWIN & FLENTKE
4.) ISSAC KNOWLES
5.) TIMOTHY RIGBY & COMPANY
6.) A.J. MARKS & COMPANY
7.) AGNER, FOUTTS & COMPANY
8.) BAGGOTT BROTHERS
9.) MANLEY, CARTWRIGHT & COMPANY
10.) HARKER POTTERY
11.) WILLIAM BRUNT
12.) McDEVITT, COCHRAN & COMPANY
13.) LAUGHLIN & SIMMS
14.) BRUNT KNOBS WORKS
15.) C.C. THOMPSON

EAST-
LIVERPOOL
(Liverpool Township)
1870

41

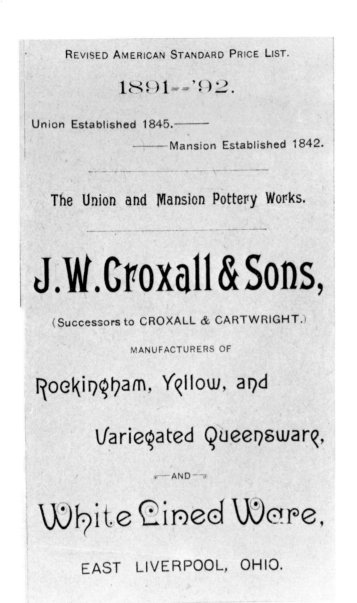

1891-1892 price catalogue cover from J. W. Croxall & Sons. Note longevity of firm represented by the founding dates of both the Union and Mansion Potteries. East Liverpool Museum of Ceramics Archives.

During the 1860s and 1870s, two marks have been found on Rockingham pieces produced by this firm. The first was an impressed mark in a circle, with "Etruria Works/East Liverpool" forming the outside of the circle and the year "1862" in the middle. The second mark was again in the form of an impressed circle reading "Etruria Works/G S Harker and Co./East Liverpool O". Although the output of yellow ware and Rockingham stopped in 1879, this firm produced white wares and semi-vitreous dinnerware well into the 20th century, establishing one of the longest records of continuous pottery production in the United States. In 1931 the company, which had been incorporated in 1888 as the Harker Pottery Company, moved from its original site in East Liverpool to Chester, West Virginia, where the owners took over the Edwin M. Knowles China Company.[6] The Harker dynasty finally closed its doors in 1972.

Although Harker's pottery had a vast history, the opposite can be said of the next pottery to appear in East Liverpool. The owners, James Salt and Frederick Mear, are the most elusive to the archivist and researcher. The knowledge that they did have a pottery from 1842-1850 has been confirmed. However, aside from the fact that they did manufacture signed pieces of yellow ware and maintained the Mansion Pottery, little is known of these two. At present an octagonal cuspidor with "Salt and Mear" impressed on the front is housed in the East Liverpool Museum of Ceramics.

The year 1844 saw two of the most powerful potteries come into being under the direction of Thomas Croxall and John Goodwin respectively. The Croxall Pottery, later known as the Union Pottery, has the distinction of being the last pottery to produce yellow ware and Rockingham exclusively throughout its history, from 1844-1910.

The Croxall history began with the arrival of Thomas Croxall in East Liverpool in 1843 from England to work for the Bennett Brothers. From the notes of Lucille Cox, which appeared in *The East Liverpool Review* on May 6, 1942, one can get a glimpse of the young Croxall's time with Bennett. "My wages amounted to $2.50 a week and I work from 7 in the morning until 6 at night. I was employed in the Bennett Pottery for 6 month and all I received during that time did not amount to more than $3. The firm sold its product to farmers in exchange for apples, potatoes, and other produce and we received most of our pay in these commodities." The idea of bartering for goods has been substantiated by a note written by James Bennett to R. Holmes on July 27, 1842. The note asks Mr. Holmes for superfine flour in exchange for pottery.

By 1844 Croxall sent for his father and three brothers and took over the Bennett Pottery. The Croxall family produced yellow ware and Rockingham until the pottery was destroyed during the great flood of 1852. In 1856 the family was back in business with Joseph Cartwright and Jonathan Kinsey in the old Union Pottery building. After 2½ years,

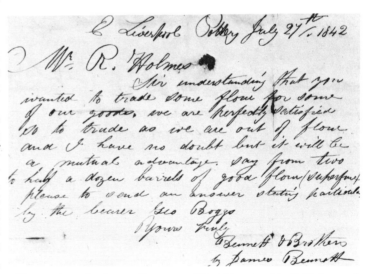

Note written by James Bennett of East Liverpool to R. Holmes of the same, to barter flour for pottery in 1842. East Liverpool Museum of Ceramics Archives.

42

Thomas Croxall and Kinsey left the firm and its name was changed to Croxall and Cartwright. The firm continued to produce yellow ware and Rockingham. In 1863 the owners bought the Mansion Pottery formerly owned by Salt and Mear; and by 1876 they were one of the largest potteries in East Liverpool.

In 1888 Croxall took over Cartwright's interest in the pottery and brought his sons George and Joseph into the firm. The name of the company was changed to J.W. Croxall and Sons. In 1898 the firm was incorporated, and became Croxall Pottery Company. In 1914 the company was sold to the American Porcelain Co.

The yellow ware line produced by this company was indeed extensive as viewed from an 1891 J.W. Croxall and Sons catalogue. Being produced at this time were nappies in 10 sizes from 3" to 12". The large nappies are now referred to as milk bowls. But it would seem from catalogue photos that milk pans, unlike nappies, had slightly rolled lips, while the standard nappy has flared sides with straight lips. The catalogue shows three sizes of custards, 5 sizes of covered butter pots with elephant-eared handles, 3 sizes of handled mugs, 5 sizes of mocha-banded pitchers, 2 sizes of French bedpans, 5 graduated, lipped, impressed bowls, 5 sizes of pie plates from 7" to 11", 12 sizes of bowls with one large white band, 4 milk pans, decorated, mocha-banded covered and uncovered chamber pots, 7 sizes of oval bakers' pans from 6" to 12", and 7 sizes of square nappies from 6" to 12".

In the manufacturing of this yellow ware, the only signature found is an impressed top of a half circle with the words "Croxall and Cartwright/East/ Liverpool/Ohio" appearing on four lines in the half circle.

At the same time that Croxall was beginning his career as a potter, John Goodwin was migrating from Burslem, England to East Liverpool via New Orleans and Cincinnati. He arrived at the Bennett Pottery in 1842 and soon was working for Harker. By 1843 it would seem that he entered into a short partnership with William Croxall and Edward Tunnicliff, but produced inferior goods due to primitive equipment and his experiments with heat intensity.[7]

Striking out on his own during the same year, he rented the Blakely Building and converted it into the Eagle Pottery, where he immediately began to produce both yellow ware and Rockingham. This pottery remained in business until 1853, when Goodwin sold it to Samuel and William Baggot and left pottery production for the next ten years. It is evident, however, through old records and price catalogues from the 1850s that the Eagle Pottery was prolific in their production of yellow ware. From an 1850 price catalogue it was noted that Goodwin produced chamberpots, pitchers, bowls, milk pans, flower pots, dishes, nappies and pie plates. An article appearing in the *Bulletin of the American Ceramic Society* suggests that the quality of the goods may have left something to be desired. "Goodwin made yellow ware and Rockingham so thick and heavy that a breakfast cup could be used in lieu of a carpenter's hammer".[8]

EAST LIVERPOOL, OHIO, 1850.

JOHN GOODWIN presents this as the lowest list of QUEESWARE PRICES in America.
(Each Kind—Twelve Pieces to the Dozen.)

NAMES. (YELLOW WARE.)			PRICES.	NAMES. (ROCKINGHAM WARE.)				PRICES.
6's Chambers,		-	$1 20	24's Pressed Pitchers,				$ 60
9's do		-	90	30's do do				50
12's do		-	60	4's Turned do				2 70
4's Pitchers,		-	1 80	6's do do				1 80
6's do		-	1 20	12's do do				90
12's do		-	60	24's do do				50
24's do		-	30	30's do do				40
30's do		-	25	4's Butter Tubs,				4 50
4's Bowls & Milk Pans,			1 80	6's do do				3 00
6's do do	do		1 20	12's do do				1 50
9's do do	do		80	6's Flower Pots,				3 00
12's do do	do		60	12's do do				1 50
24's do do	do		30	12's Honey Bowls,				1 50
30's do do	do		25	6's Turned Washbowls,				1 80
36's do do	do		20	6's Turned Ewers,				1 80
4's Butter Tubs,			3 00	4's Pres'd Ewers Bowls,				7 20
6's do			2 00	6's do do	do			4 80
12's do	do		1 00	6's Coffee Pots,				4 00
6's Flower Pots,			2 00	4's do do				6 00
12's do	do		1 00	18's Pressed Tea-Pots,				2 00
24's Mugs,		-	30	18's do Sugars,				1 60
30's do		-	25	30's do Creams,				50
36's do		-	20	18's Turned Tea-Pots,				2 00
12 inch Dishes & Napies,			1 20	24's do do				1 50
11 " do	do		1 00	30's do Sugars,				1 25
10 " do	do		80	30's do Creams,				40
9 " do	do		60	Bed Pans,		-		4 00
8 " do	do		50	Salid Dishes,		-		1 00
7 " do	do		40	10inch Spittoons,		-		3 00
6 " do	do		30	9 " do		-		2 50
10 " Pie-Plates,			50	8 " do		-		2 00
9 " do			40	7 " do		-		1 50
8 " do			30	5 " Sauce Dishes,				30
7 " do			25	6 " do do				40
ROCKINGHAM WARE.				7 " do do				55
4's Pressed Pitchers,			$3 60	8 " do do				70
6's do	do		2 40	9 " do do				85
12's do	do		1 20	10 " do do				1 00

W. L. CLARKE, Printer, Wellsville, Ohio.   Patronage respectfully solicited.

Early price list from the Goodwin Pottery demonstrating sales technique of having the lowest prices in America. Shows there must have been much competition in the field of yellow ware production. East Liverpool Museum of Ceramics Archives.

In 1863, Goodwin returned to the world of pottery and established the Novelty Pottery Works, which he sold within 2 years to A.J. Marks and Co. By 1870 Goodwin surfaced in Trenton, New Jersey, and held an interest in the Trenton Pottery Co. In 1872 he returned to East Liverpool and purchased the Broadway Pottery. The company, already set up for the manufacture of yellow ware, immediately began production with the aid of Goodwin's three sons: James, George, and Henry. The name of the company became John Goodwin and Sons. By the time Goodwin died in 1875, the company was producing a strong line of yellow ware.

An 1875 catalogue shows evidence that the line was not only strong, but exceedingly varied. The company produced oval bakers, pressed bowls in 7 sizes ranging from 12½" and 5¼", turned bowls, lipped bowls, covered butter jars, bedpans, birdbaths, chambers, nappies in 9 sizes from

9″ to 5″, turned jugs, round and oval jelly moulds, jelly cans, milk pans in 4 sizes from 14″ to 10″, mugs, pie plates, swan tobacco jars, round custard or cake cups, round soap drainers and round cake bakers.

After the death of their father, the three brothers continued to run the company, but changed the name to Goodwin Brothers Pottery Company. They produced yellow ware and Rockingham for a short while and then converted the plant for the production of white ware. The company reincorporated as the Goodwin Pottery Company in 1893, and finally ended their dynasty in 1913.

An interesting footnote to the Goodwin saga takes on a twentieth century air. Squire Hill of East Liverpool recorded in 1847 that partnership papers had been drawn up and signed by Goodwin, establishing his wife, Ester Smith Goodwin, as an equal partner in the John Goodwin Pottery Co.[9]

There is an abundance of information concerning the next potter to appear in East Liverpool, one named Jabez Vodrey. Due to an in-depth personal diary and family remembrances, Vodrey becomes at times larger than life. Born in 1795 in Staffordshire, England, Vodrey received a fine education in the art of pottery making in France, Tunstall, Staffordshire, Brampton, and Derbyshire, then left his motherland. He arrived in Baltimore, Maryland on March 10, 1827.

Once established in Pittsburgh, he teamed up with William Frost and began to produce clay. Spargo states that he was located in East Liberties or Liberties, but from an obituary of his son, William Henry Vodrey, it would seem the business was located at "Old Fourth Street Road, now Fifth Avenue Extension."[10] Only one piece of pottery survives that is known to have come from this pottery. It is a cream-colored sugar bowl lid which is housed at the East Liverpool Museum of Ceramics.

Abandoning the Pittsburgh area in 1829 or 1830, Vodrey and Frost traveled to Louisville, Kentucky to work for the Lewis Pottery. Within three years, Frost left the concern, and died in 1835. By 1832 contracts were signed naming Vodrey as turner and his brother-in-law as thrower for the Lewis Company. From further family documents it would seem that two children died in Louisville and 3 others were born: William Henry Vodrey in 1832, James Norman Vodrey in 1834 and John Wadsworth Vodrey in 1836.

By 1839 Vodrey moved to Troy, Indiana; where he worked for the Indiana Pottery Company, known for their production of Rockingham. This venture was abandoned in 1846; and by the following year, 1847 Vodrey appeared in East Liverpool.

Here Vodrey began to make a name for himself by producing clay pots, but within a year he formed a partnership with William Woodward for the production of yellow ware and Rockingham. The pottery was soon destroyed by fire. Two new partners, James and John S. Blakely, were found in 1853, and the firm became known as Woodward, Blakely and Co. Their main production was that of yellow ware, Rockingham and terra cotta. This new venture was large, with the firm producing perhaps the

Covered yellow ware jar or pot attributed to the Vodrey Pottery. Unusual in that no finial seen on lid. East Liverpool Museum of Ceramics Collection, Ohio.

greatest amount of yellow ware in the 1850s. The company was even successful enough to maintain a showroom in Pittsburgh. Problems, however, racked the company, and by 1858 the once-powerful Phoenix Pottery was defunct.

In 1857 Vodrey's three sons set out to convert an old church into a pottery. By 1858, the Vodrey and Brothers Pottery Company was born. The pottery was named Palissy Works, and began a twenty-year production of yellow ware and Rockingham. In 1861 Vodrey died, leaving his 3 sons to run the business and produce yellow ware until 1876. The pottery legacy of the Vodreys did not die there, for it was reported that as late as 1938, William Norman Vodrey, grandson of Jabez Vodrey, was the superintendent of the Thompson Pottery Co. of East Liverpool, representing 100 years of pottery history.

By 1858, the firm was established as the Vodrey Bros., and continued to carry the name Palissy Pottery Works. Although they only produced yellow ware and Rockingham until 1876, their 1870 price catalogue emphasizes their yellow ware, Rockingham and white-lined ware. In production at this time were pressed bowls, bedpans, birdbaths, soap drainers, custards, lipped bowls, square bakers in 7 sizes from 5 to 12 inches, round-rimmed bakers in six sizes from 7 to 12 inches, pie plates in four sizes, mugs, milk pans, nappies in 9 sizes from 4 to 12 inches, scalloped nappies in 6 sizes from 4 to 9 inches, jelly cans, butter pots, chambers and pitchers.

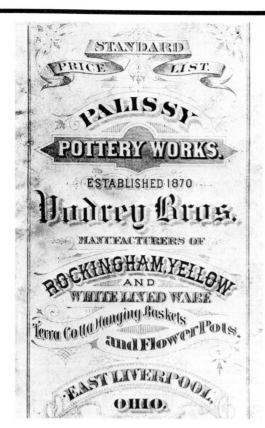

Cover of Palissy Pottery Works price catalogue. Owned and operated by Vodrey Brothers of East Liverpool, Ohio. Note they not only produced Rockingham and yellow ware but a white-lined yellow ware, as did England. East Liverpool Museum of Ceramics Archives.

1864 price list from Vodrey Pottery Works. East Liverpool Museum of Ceramics Archives.

Through studying the histories of potters, quite frequently an important bit of information arises that helps to confirm or deny previous speculations. The Vodrey papers do just that in answering the question "did American yellow ware ever have white interior linings?" For years experts on the subject have asserted that white-lined yellow ware was foreign. Vodrey explodes this myth in his annuals, discussing the production of a yellow ware mocha-banded mug with white lining and a yellow ware frog inside. The East Liverpool Museum houses such a piece, and correctly attributes it to Vodrey. It remains an unfortunate fact that many collectors may be passing up superior pieces such as this due to the myth about the foreign origin of white-lined pieces. Perhaps now, thanks to Vodrey and his writings, the collector will be more at ease to purchase a white-lined piece. It should be noted that some English yellow ware may have had white linings, but American pieces also used this ceramic innovation.

Yellow ware was next produced in East Liverpool by William Brunt, who by 1848 went into partnership with his son-in-law, William Bloor. By 1853 Bloor left the pottery, and Brunt turned to his two sons, Henry and William Jr., to establish William Brunt and Brothers in 1856. In 1859 William Jr. left the firm to establish his own pottery. He purchased the Phoenix Pottery, which had belonged to Woodward, Blakely and Co. He began his production of yellow ware in 1860, and when his brother-in-law, William

Bloor, left his pottery, Brunt purchased it and combined the two potteries into one huge operation. The Civil War damaged this growing concern, and Brunt sold half of his firm, comprising the original building, to John Thompson, William Jobling, James Taylor and John Hardwick in 1865. The name "Phoenix", however, stayed with Brunt; and the new owners renamed their part of the Brunt operation Lincoln Pottery. Brunt produced yellow ware until 1877, when he reconstructed his factory for the production of white ware.

From an 1865 price list of the Wm. Brunt Jr. and Co., known as the Phoenix Pottery Works, one learns that he produced round-rim bakers, nappies, pie plates, butter pots, cake pans, chambers, embossed chambers, pitchers in 3 patterns: plain, parian and tulip, plain bowls, pressed and embossed bowls, lipped bowls, pressed-lipped bowls, jelly cans, bedpans, mugs, washbowls, snuff jars, and pound-cake pans. As if his production line was not enough, in 1867 Brunt joined his brother Henry and H.R. Hill to form the Hill, Brunt and Co. Pottery, which was called the "Great Western Pottery Works". The pottery produced yellow ware and Rockingham until 1874. The Brunt dynasty remained alive until 1911.

In contrast to the large and wide-spread Brunt Co. and its affiliates, the next pottery to be discussed was small and unknown. Information on Richard Harrison and Co., formed in 1852, is vague. What brings him to light at all is a

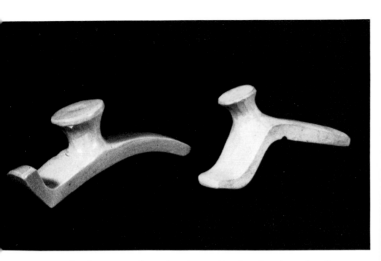

Pair of yellow ware hand tools used in the shaping of yellow ware bowls. These came out of the Vodrey Pottery. East Liverpool Museum of Ceramics Collection, Ohio.

piece of Rockingham signed "Richard Harrison and Co./figural propeller/East/Liverpool/Ohio" in a raised medallion impressed on the piece. The pottery was short-lived, and within a few years it was purchased by Alex Young. Besides the 1850 census that establishes Richard Harrison as a potter in East Liverpool, not much is known.

Not all people who came to East Liverpool were in the pottery business. However, many sooner or later became part of that growing phenomenon. One such person was Isaac Watts Knowles, who came to East Liverpool in the 1830s as a carpenter. It has been stated that he became the first pottery salesman in the area working for James Bennett. Knowles built a boat, and loaded with yellow ware, sailed down the Ohio River onto the Mississippi and into New Orleans selling his wares. The venture was reported as totally unsuccessful.[11] For the next thirteen years, Knowles built equipment for the potteries in East Liverpool.

After the floods of 1852 that nearly devastated East Liverpool, Knowles built the East Liverpool Pottery. In 1854 he began to produce yellow ware and Rockingham with a partner, Isaac Harvey. Their main product was a line of ceramic self-sealing canning jars. Harvey left the business in the mid-1860s, and due to the advent of glass canning jars, the business began to collapse. By 1870 Knowles enlisted the aid of his son Homer and his son-in-law John N. Taylor, to form the Knowles, Taylor, and Knowles Co., which continued to produce yellow ware and Rockingham until 1876, when Knowles began to re-equip his pottery for the production of white ware. The business finally closed its doors in 1929.

The 1850s continued to see great growth in East Liverpool, despite the flood of 1852 and the recession of 1857. The next pottery to emerge was the Salamander Pottery Works, owned by William Flentke, George and Samuel Morley, James Goodwin and David Colclough.

An 1865-1866 price catalogue from Wm. Brunt Jr. & Co. showing Rockingham and yellow ware prices. Note name given to yellow ware: "Yellow Queensware". East Liverpool Museum of Ceramics Archives.

They leased the Henderson Pottery in 1855, and by 1857 they owned the building and were producing yellow ware and Rockingham. By 1861 both Colclough and S. Morley left the firm; and by 1874 Morley, Goodwin, and Flentke built a large building across from the Salamander Works for the production of white ware. They retained the name "Salamander" but discontinued the production of yellow ware. The old building was taken over by Worchester and Flentke and renamed the Buckeye Pottery. Their prime production was yellow ware and Rockingham. By 1881 this

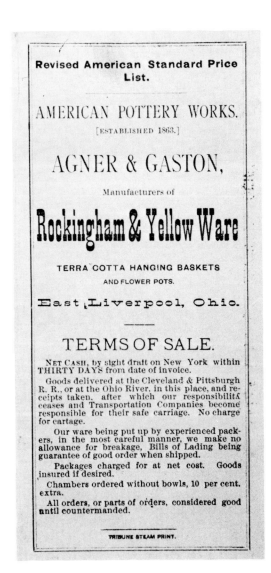

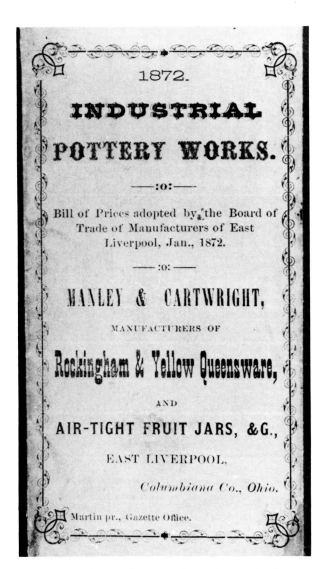

Cover of American Pottery Works, established in 1863. This company was short-lived but produced a viable line of yellow ware. East Liverpool Museum of Ceramics Archives.

1872 catalogue of prices from Manley & Cartwright. Once again, yellow ware called "Yellow Queensware". East Liverpool Museum of Ceramics Archives.

pottery was sold to Knowles, Taylor and Knowles for the production of ironstone. Entering the 1860s East Liverpool felt the wrath of the Civil War. The pottery industry held on, but new business was short-lived or fluctuating at the time. Those involved in the sixties were Henry Speeler, who began his work with Harker, and then travelled back and forth to New Jersey: William Bloor, who returned to East Liverpool from New Jersey in 1859 to buy part of the Phoenix Pottery Company that belonged to Woodward and Blakely; Agner and Gaston, who established a yellow ware pottery in 1863; Manley and Cartwright, who established a yellow ware firm in 1864; and the Laughlin Brothers, Homer and Shakespeare, who would lay the foundation of a ceramic dynasty in 1868 by selling yellow ware and Rockingham. The sixties were volatile times for the entire country; yet East Liverpool continued to manufacture and distribute its wares. William Bloor lost interest in yellow ware on his return to Ohio, and helped create the first white ware works in East Liverpool. These new white ware works would allow the town to prosper well into the 1930s.

Little is known at present about the Agner and Gaston Co. that opened in 1863. It changed ownership in 1868, with Foults replacing Gaston, but continued to produce yellow ware. Their product line included nappies, bakers, figured and pressed bowls, lipped bowls, chambers and jelly cans, cake pans, milk pans, stove tubs, scalloped dishes, butter pots, mugs, pie plates, birdbaths, airtight butter jars in 2 quart through 6 quart sizes.

In 1864, just before the end of the Civil War, Holland Manley and William Cartwright purchased the Webster Stoneware Pottery, which they soon enlarged and named Industrial Pottery Works. They produced a fine line of yellow ware until 1887. In production were plain and pressed lipped bowls, bedpans, chamberpots from 7″ to 10″, 2 sizes of bean pots, jelly cans, milk and cake pans, butter pots in 5 sizes from a pint to a gallon, stove tubs, oval bakers, mugs in 3 sizes, pie plates, scalloped rice dishes in 5 sizes from 5″ to 9″, airtight fruit jars and airtight fruit jars with tin-labeled covers.

Cover of C.C. Thompson Pottery Company catalogue. East Liverpool Museum of Ceramics Archives.

By the end of 1860s, with the Civil War over and the economy getting back on its feet, East Liverpool again saw a surge of new potteries being built. In 1868 C.C. Thompson and J.T. Herbert built a small pottery for the production of yellow ware, Rockingham and semi-granite ware. Within 2 years Herbert was bought out by Thompson's father and Basil Simms; and the company became known as C.C. Thompson and Co. Expansion was quick and by 1881 the company employed some 200 workers.[48] From an 1886 catalogue one finds the yellow ware production to be ample, although not foremost in the company line. Catalogue entries included nappies, scalloped dish nests, chambers, pie plates, bakers and bowls.

Incorporated as the C.C. Thompson Pottery Company in 1889 after the death Josiah Thompson, the firm continued to produce yellow ware and Rockingham. According to a company price catalogue, under the new name, the yellow ware line was refined and expanded. By the 1890s the C.C. Thompson Pottery Co. was producing nested custards in 3 sizes, nested nappies in 11 sizes from 3″ to 13″, nested pie plates in 4 sizes from 7″ to 10″, 4 sizes of banded butter jars from 2 pints to 8 pints, pressed-lipped bowls, nested banded bowl sets in 11 sizes from 5″ to 17″, oval bakers in 7 sizes from 6″ to 12″, four sizes of banded mugs, jelly moulds in 4 sizes, turned mocha-banded jugs in 5 sizes, shovel-shaped bedpans, toy or mini-banded chambers, and mocha-banded covered and uncovered chambers in 4 sizes from 7″ to 10″.

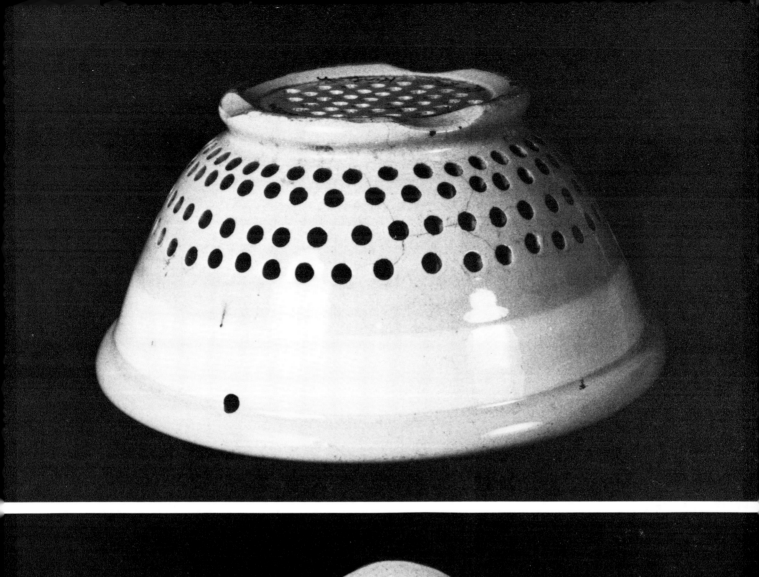
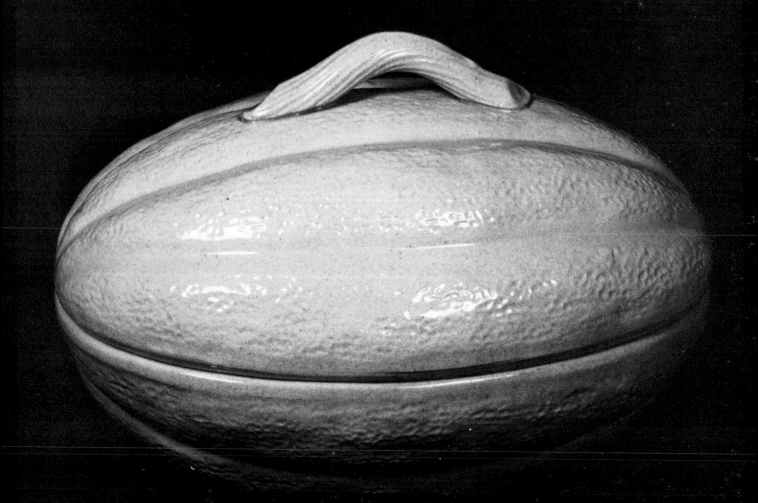

Unusual yellow ware teapot, molded basketweave design. Definitely an Ohio piece, however, could easily be attributed to England. Attributed to the C.C. Thompson Co. and used for a baking soda company promotion. East Liverpool Museum Ceramics Collection, Ohio.

Most unusual frog mug showing seaweed banding and white interior. Definitely Ohio attributed to Vodrey. Should put an end to the theory that all such pieces are English! East Liverpool Museum of Ceramics Collection, Ohio.

Although no impressed signatures were found on these yellow wares, in 1905 a paper label was used which read "The C.C. Thompson Pottery Co./manufacturer of/Semi-Granite/C.C. and Decorated Ware/Rockingham and Yellow ware/East Liverpool, Ohio."[13] The firm continued to manufacture yellow ware until 1917.

In 1875 the Star Pottery, under the direction of Bulger and Worchester, was formed and lasted until 1888. Little is known about this company. It was short-lived but productive, with an inventory of yellow ware, Rockingham and terra cotta. From an 1879 price catalogue, we learn the firm produced oval bakers, rice or scalloped dishes, opened and closed chambers, bedpans, pie plates, milk pans, mugs, nappies, stove tubs, covered butter pots in 4 sizes from 1 quart to 1 gallon, pressed and turned bowls in 10 sizes from 5" to 14", lipped bowls and birdbaths. No marks were used to identify this ware.

Most unusual pieces attributed to Frederich, Shenkle & Allen of the Globe Pottery Co., East Liverpool. A footed yellow ware teapot with a raised strawberry and vine design and a molded yellow ware pitcher with colored panel designs.

Rare octagonal yellow ware spittoon, with molded decorations and company name, Salt and Mear, displayed on piece. East Liverpool Museum Collection, Ohio.

51

Catalogue page from D.E. McNichol Pottery Co. showing their production line of Rock-ingham and yellow ware. Here one can see clearly the difference in shape between a nappy and milk pan. East Liverpool Museum of Ceramics Archives.

In 1881 a retired grocer named Shenkle joined N.A. Frederick and A.B. Allen to form the Frederick, Shenkle, Allen Co. The Globe Pottery Company emerged from this company in 1888, and was in existence until 1901. The company began the production of yellow ware in 1882, but by 1887 were re-equiping the company to produce white ware. In 1901 Globe merged with East Liverpool Potteries Company, but was reinstated as the Globe Pottery in 1907 with the failure of the E.L. Potteries Co. By this time the transition from yellow ware to white ware had been completed; and the company produced semi-porcelains. During the years of yellow ware production, the company was known for its figurals, such as elephants.

Only one mark has been found to identify Globe wares. The mark used was a stamped circle with a globe stamped in the center and the words "THE GLOBE POTTERY/EAST LIVERPOOL" around the globe. This signature was found on pieces made between 1888-1901.

The transition from yellow to white wares began in the late 1870s. By the 1890s it was necessary for those yellow ware firms still in existence to either make a transition from yellow ware to white ware or at least produce both wares in order to survive. The mood and refinement of American tastes had spoken. The transition of the Globe Pottery was important enough to be written about in the *Illustrated Glass and Pottery World*, January 1897. "...just in the midst of changing part of its plant to producing white granite and new buildings have also been put up. It will be the first of February before it will be ready to fill orders for granite. In the meantime it is well stocked with cane colored and rock wares...."

The firm of McNichol, Burton and Co., which originated in 1869, is mentioned here as a forerunner of the D.E. McNichol Pottery Co. It was made up of 7 enterprising men who in 1869 bought the Novelty Pottery which belonged to A.J. Marks and began the production of yellow ware and Rockingham. By 1875 John Dover retired, and John

Mini sugar bowl molded in the English tradition and attributed to McNichol, 1892-1925. East Liverpool Museum of Ceramics Collection, Ohio.

McNichol sold his interest to his sons, Daniel and H.A. The firm continued to expand by the mid-1880s the Burtons left the firm. Eighteen ninety-two saw Daniel Edward McNichol take over the company, changing its name to the D.E. McNichol Pottery Co. Continuing to expand, the company produced yellow ware and Rockingham until 1929 and a full line of semi-granite ware until 1954. Although no marks have been found, the company was known for the production of nappies, bowls, impressed lipped bowls, custards, banded butters, pie plates and milk pans.

D.E. McNichol, producing yellow ware well into the mid-20th century, was the last firm in East Liverpool to do so. Bowls from this company show 20th century lips and collars much more bulbous than previously seen.

The John Patterson and Sons Pottery Company began production of yellow ware and Rockingham in 1883 at 12th and Anderson Avenue, Wellsville, Ohio. In the pottery world, Wellsville is considered part of East Liverpool.

Production continued until 1900, when the firm became Patterson Brothers Co. From 1900 to 1917 they produced yellow ware, Rockingham, cream-colored wares, and low-end semi-vitreous chinas. In 1917 the company was sold to the Sterling China Co. No marks have been found.

Among its wares, the company produced soup dishes, teapots, mugs, cups, humidors, nappies and bowls. During this time, yellow ware was taking on a more formal and delicate style. Humidors with banded lids and bodies and teacups without handles with a blotched glaze applied were produced. Although with technology yellow ware became more decorative in motif and form, it also became less available because these new processes could be used on the more popular white wares and on porcelains as well. Technology was for yellow ware a two-edged sword; it enhanced its look, but at the same time it caused a decline in its production.

Yellow ware humidor with mocha seaweed bands attributed to McNichol & Burton c. 1856. Most unusual piece. East Liverpool Museum of Ceramics Collection, Ohio.

Magnificent trade sign exhibiting yellow ware with flint enamel decoration applied. Might be considered a ceramic calling card for Harker & Thompson, East Liverpool. East Liverpool Museum Ceramics Collection, Ohio.

Three motifs used to decorate yellow ware. The 3 pieces are attributed to John Patterson Sons, and Croxall.

Seaweed-banded colander, Ohio. East Liverpool Museum of Ceramics Collection, Ohio.

Small collection of green and brown spattered yellow ware. Found mostly in Ohio. Milk pitcher shows typical Ohio design.

Yellow ware spatter-decorated pie plate, found mostly in Ohio production. Done with greens and browns, can be found with blue, but less common due to cost of blue oxide.

MUSKINGUM COUNTY

Sitting on the Muskingum River, Muskingum County has a strong history in flint and clay production dating back to the Mound Builders and the Wyandot Indians. The abundance of its production came from Zanesville, which sits on the river by the Muskingum Falls. With vast clay deposits, transportation routes and hydraulic power from the falls, Zanesville had attracted many of the Staffordshire potters by the 1840s, and the pottery industry grew rapidly. Known as early as 1808 for its production of redware by Samuel Sullivan, who is believed to have established the first true pottery in the area, the county became known in the 19th century for its Rockingham and stoneware, and in the 20th century for its Roseville Pottery.

One of the earliest potteries to produce yellow ware belonged to Bernard Howson, John Hallam and George Wheaton. These three men arrived in Zanesville in 1840 and began to produce yellow ware and brown ware. They brought with them secrets such as Rockingham, and began to manufacture what they called "American Rockingham".[14] It should be noted that at the same time East Liverpool was producing Rockingham. Rockingham, it would seem, was the major product in Zanesville, although we know from research that yellow ware was indeed made and sold. Howson, Hallam, and Wheaton made pie plates, soap dishes, toothbrush holders, mugs, pitchers, toilet articles, foot warmers, asthma inhalers, bedpans, flasks in the shape of books, spittoons and dogs. No marks have been found that can be attributed to this company.

Howson soon left his Staffordshire friends to strike out on his own, taking his son John as a partner. They produced a crude line of yellow ware and by 1863, Bernard died, leaving the company in John's hands. John ran the operation from 1863-1874. There was a steady decline in the quality of the wares produced, and by 1874 the company was producing ink bottles. Shortly afterward, a New York firm bought the factory and turned to the production of flooring and faience tiles.[15] No marks have been found on Howson pieces.

The premier potter of Zanesville was George Pyatt, a leading force in the area for twenty years. He arrived from England to establish a yellow ware and Rockingham factory in 1849 which produced wares superior in design and workmanship. He formed a partnership with Christopher Getz in 1851, which dissolved two years later when Getz pulled up stakes for Cincinnati. It is believed that he had a hand in establishing many potteries in that area.

In 1859 Pyatt and three other potters left Zanesville for Kaolin, Missouri. Unlike his previous venture with yellow ware, in Missouri he began to produce white ware. He left Missouri with the outbreak of the Civil War and returned to Zanesville, first working for Howson and then establishing himself in business in 1866. J.G. Pyatt took over the firm after the death of his father in 1879, and renamed the company the Tremont Pottery, which remained in existence until 1900.

Barrel-shaped caning jar from the D.E. McNichol Company 1892-1925. East Liverpool Museum of Ceramics Collection, Ohio.

Other potters to produce yellow ware and Rockingham in the area were:
Joseph Rambo, 1863-c.1870
Alfred Wilber, North Ward Pottery, 1873-1878
Calvin Bumbaugh, Star Pottery, 1873-1900
Duncan Hamelback, 1874-c.1880
N.K. Smith, 1878
Jacob S. King and John T. Swope, 1879-1900

CINCINNATI

Located on the north bank of the Ohio River, Cincinnati became an important transportation town early in the 1800s. By 1811 steamboat service began on the river, and Cincinnati became a prime trade location. With local transportation routes, the city became a link to northern Ohio once the Erie Canal was developed, and, to the south when the Civil War ended. With trade routes in place and an abundance of clay on the banks of the river, what better place to establish potteries. By the 1830s the population of Cincinnati was around 25,000 and the demand for utilitarian wares was great. Known for its redware and stoneware, and later as an innovator of decorated ware leading to the birth of Art Pottery, Cincinnati had only a brief love affair with yellow ware.

Although detailed information on yellow ware potters remains scant at this time, a general theme can be established. With the exception of a few pioneer potters before the mid-1800s, production of yellow ware seems to have run from 1850 to the late 1870s and early 1880s. No potters marks have been found. This omission is logical, because yellow ware was not the major ware produced in Cincinnati. Most of the time slots which follow must be viewed as circa dates, for there are at least three conflicting dates for many of the potters.

Ohio milk pitchers. Many of these were used as advertising pieces
for stores and restaurants.

Yellow ware with mocha seaweed band applied. Shows semi-
turned lip and applied handle. Ohio. East Liverpool Museum of
Ceramics Collection, Ohio.

Wonderful example of turks head mould, unusual to find in yellow ware. Mostly seen in redware. East Liverpool Museum of Ceramics Collection, Ohio.

Inkwells, both yellow ware, one displaying a blue overglaze. Yellow ware dog in foreground attributed to Vodrey, c. 1870. East Liverpool Museum of Ceramics Collection, Ohio.

Funnel made in yellow ware produced by McNichol, and often sold with preserve jars. East Liverpool Museum of Ceramics Collection, Ohio.

The honors of maintaining the first pottery in Cincinnati have traditionally gone to the Kendall family, beginning with Uriah Kendall, who was thought to have produced stoneware. It is doubtful that he made yellow ware. If the dates are correct, James Doane, c.1831-1837 was the first yellow ware pottery in Cincinnati. The Kendall family may have started producing yellow ware in 1846, when Uriah Kendall's son came into the business, and the name was changed to Kendall and Sons. Little is known of this company except that by 1850 it seems to have disappeared; and the family moved further west.

William Bromley arrived in Cincinnati in 1842, but did not start a pottery until 1849. From the Cincinnati Directory it would seem that he opened the Brighton Pottery on Hamilton Street. Throughout his career as a potter, Bromley either expanded his works or moved twice more. He moved to Western Row in 1857 when he took on a partner: Joseph Bailey. This partnership was short-lived, and by 1860 the Brighton Pottery was again listed at the Hamilton Street address with Bromley's son as a partner. The address then changed to Central Avenue, but it would seem that this was merely an expansion of the original site.

George Scott was the next potter to produce yellow ware in Cincinnati. There is much confusion as to the dates that George Scott was in business. For the purpose of continuity, it can be assumed once again from city directories that Scott may have arrived in Cincinnati around 1846, and began his career in the pottery world as an agent for

Bromley. By 1853 he is listed in the city directory as a maker of yellow ware and Rockingham, having established a pottery on Front Street. In 1889 his son joined the firm, which remained in business until 1901.

Not much information has been gathered about another Cincinnati potter, Henry Mappes. The Cincinnati Directory establishes him at the Vine Street Pottery at two addresses on Vine Street in 1857. By 1875 this site was not only a factory but also a sales office. By 1880 the company included Henry Mappes's brother; and by 1884 the company moved its facilities to Chester Park Station and changed its name to the Chester Park Pottery. Flowerpots, stovepipes, and yellow ware were produced.

One of the most famous potters in Cincinnati, Samuel Pollack began his Dayton Street Pottery in 1859, making yellow ware and Rockingham. Upon his death in 1870, his family took over the business until 1874, when Patrick Coultry assumed ownership. Coultry began to transfer his ceramic endeavors into the making of "Cincinnati Faience",[16] which was to revolutionize the pottery industry of Cincinnati. Cincinnati Faience allowed the city to grow to become the Art Pottery Capital of the United States. After the initial rage, however, Coultry found his wares hard to sell. In an effort to save his business, he continued to produce yellow ware. But in 1883, he was forced to close his doors.

More confusion reigns over the dates that Tempest, Brockmann and Co. was productive. It would seem that the

Bedpan produced in Ohio, one of two styles in production. East Liverpool Museum of Ceramics Collection, Ohio.

company began to produce a common yellow ware in 1862, but this was short-lived, for in 1867 the company was already producing white ware and cream ware. By 1881 the name had been changed to the Tempest, Brockmann and Sampson Pottery. In 1887 C.E. Brockmann bought out the stockholders, and the company became the Brockmann Pottery Co.

The Dallas Pottery, active from 1865-1882, was originally owned by M. and N. Tempest, but by 1865 it was in the hands of Frederick Dallas. He continued to produce yellow ware, brown fruit jars and Rockingham for four years after he purchased the firm, but then refitted his works to produce white ware and cream ware.

It should be noted that the Dallas Pottery began the art pottery craze that would soon take over the pottery world and allow Cincinnati to flourish.

Between 1848 and 1859, Cincinnati witnessed a large outcropping of yellow ware makers, although most were short-lived. With the present sparsity of information it must suffice to list these potters until more information surfaces.

1848-1899 Lessel Family
1848-1852 Peter Lessel
1852-1879 Peter Lessel and Bro.
1879-1899 George Lessel
1854 Brewer and Tempest
1854-1856 Hamlet Greatbach
1855-1857 Valentine Eichenlaub

1856-1859 Tunis Brewer
1857-1877 Andrew Behn
1857-1900 George Peter Behn
1857-1865 M. and N. Tempest
1859-1869 J.A. Brewer[17]

The three centers of East Liverpool, Muskingum County and Cincinnati, although predominant in yellow ware production were by no means the only areas to establish yellow ware potteries. Scattered throughout the state of Ohio were other makers of yellow ware in areas such as Middlebury and Akron. For the purposes of this book, however, the three areas of East Liverpool, Muskingum County and Cincinnati must stand as the strongholds of the production of this transitional ware. Without any doubt, Ohio must be acknowledged as the mother-lode of yellow ware in the United States.

Without this transitional ware and the potters who brought their talents to this state, the continuing refinement of wares that evolved during the experimentation and production of yellow ware would not have taken place; and the ceramic industry may have collapsed. It must also be noted that Ohio, with its access not only to the north, but also to the south and west, played a significant role in setting the stage for the acceptance of "American-Made" ceramics in this country. With the advent of yellow ware, the British monopoly on ceramics began to dissolve.

Yellow ware overglazed with green and brown sponge design. Bowl demonstrates a horizontal rib design.

Spattered green and brown on molded yellow ware pitcher. Piece demonstrates applied handle. Made in Ohio. East Liverpool Museum of Ceramics Collection, Ohio.

Pair of yellow ware pitchers with brown and green sponge design. Note pale yellow bodies.

Jetware teapot, yellow ware body attributed to Croxall & Cartwright. East Liverpool Museum of Ceramics Collection, Ohio.

Early yellow ware bowl with mocha seaweed applied. Heavy in composition and poorly executed mocha band. Attributed to Salt and Mear. East Liverpool Museum of Ceramics Collection, Ohio.

CHAPTER 5

ANCILLARY PRODUCERS

Some of the most capable potters in the United States plied their trade in the New England states from the 1700s into the 1900s. When one thinks of New England pottery, one thinks stoneware and redware, not yellow ware. The production of this transitional ware is at best scant in this area. Perhaps one of the reasons for the near-absence of yellow ware was the need to import the yellow clay from Long Island and South Amboy, New Jersey. Transporation lines and costs may have entered into the scarcity of production. Whatever the reason may be, yellow ware, although produced throughout New England, was only an addendum to other wares.

VERMONT

Since Greatbach, the master modeler from New Jersey, came to Bennington, Vermont to work for Fenton, it would seem logical to begin in Vermont. The contribution here in the realm of stoneware, Rockingham, flint enamel and Scroddle ware was enormous, with workmanship that was unsurpassed. Although the Rockingham and much of the flint enamel was worked with a yellow ware base, yellow ware itself was certainly not favored in production.

In Vermont the focus of yellow ware manufacturing rests in Bennington, where Norton and Fenton produced it from 1845-1847. Soon afterward, the Lyman and Fenton Company began production from 1849-1858. Although the Nortons had an extensive history in Bennington, Vermont, the years of yellow ware production were minimal and hardly recognized. The Bennington Museum at present houses only eight pieces of yellow ware amid a huge display of Rockingham and flint enamel. Yellow ware production began in Bennington in 1841 when Julius Norton took control of his father's pottery. Included with the production of salt-glazed crocks, jugs, churns, and redware was the production of Rockingham and yellow ware.

Working for Norton at this time was Christopher Fenton, who would marry Norton's sister and by 1844, form a partnership with Norton that lasted until 1847. It has been believed that under this partnership a crude form of yellow ware was produced. This can be refuted, however, by an hexagonal pitcher on display at the Bennington Museum signed "Norton and Fenton, Bennington Vermont" that is anything but crude.

Once the company was dissolved each partner struck out on his own. Norton produced fine stoneware until 1894. Fenton continued to produce Rockingham and yellow ware, but also began to manufacture porcelains. In 1848 he took 2 partners: one, a lawyer named Lyman, and the other, a merchant named Park.[1] By November of 1849, Park left the business. The firm of Lyman and Fenton was born, and thrived until 1858. The production of Rockingham and yellow ware was continued with the aid of Daniel Greatbach, who came to Fenton from New Jersey, and master mould-maker Enoch Wood, of Staffordshire fame. The Rockingham line excelled with magnificent hound-handle pitchers, spittoons, coolers, cow pitchers and presentation pieces. By 1858 when Fenton moved and established a yellow ware, Rockingham and white ware pottery in Peoria, Illinois.

In the short period of 1844-1847, two marks were displayed on yellow ware; "Norton and Fenton/ East Bennington in 1844″ and "Norton and Fenton/ Bennington in 1844-7″. Under the Lyman and Fenton partnership, one mark was used from 1849-58: an impressed large circle with Lyman Fenton/ Fentons/ Enameled/ Patented/ 1849/ Bennington, Vermont".

The Bennington production of yellow ware included pitchers, milk pans, custards, nappies, baking dishes, pie plates, mini crocks, jugs and pitchers.

MASSACHUSETTS

In Massachusetts redware and stoneware dominated. Boston, however, was a production center for yellow ware, beginning in 1852 with the Boston Earthenware Factory until the turn of the century, when the Boston Pottery Company ended its production of yellow ware. From the Boston directory of 1893 comes the following advertising. "Boston Pottery Co./ Manufacturers of every description of/ Stoneware/ Rockingham and Yellow ware/...[2].

The Boston Earthenware Factory, 1852-1858, was established to produce yellow ware and Rockingham by Frederick Mear, who came to Boston from East Liverpool, Ohio, where he was a pioneer potter in partnership with Salt. He remained as elusive in Boston as he did in Ohio.

Following the lead of the Boston Earthenware Factory, the New England Pottery Company, 1854-75, was started by Frederick Meagher. It was later sold to Homer, and in 1875

Yellow ware poodles, tails have been mended. Detailed work in face, but overall composition is primitive. Bennington Museum Collection, Vermont.

Hexagonal pitcher exhibiting floral-paneled sides and neck designs. Applied handle styled in the English tradition. Piece marked "Norton/Fenton Bennington Vermont". c.1844-1847. Height 6¼", diameter 4" at the mouth. Bennington Museum Collection, Vermont.

Mini crocks and jugs produced as toys, and rare to any collection. Jug on left side demonstrates a green glaze over yellow ware. Produced in Bennington, Vermont. Bennington Museum Collection, Vermont.

was sold once again, to Clark and Gray. Its production of yellow ware was brief, as white ware soon replaced it.

The Boston Pottery Company, in existence from 1878-1900, was located in East Boston near Bordon Street, and was still producing yellow ware as late as 1893 according to directory information.

The Somerset Pottery, producing until 1909, was established sometime before 1886 by the Chase family, who would leave Boston for Norwich, Connecticut. An 1886 Boston directory ad read "...Manufacturers of and wholesale dealers in white, decorated, Rockingham, Yellow, Stone and Earthenware"[3]. The company was located at 39 and 40 Commercial Wharf, Boston. An interesting note arises here in that this company found a buff-colored clay at the Western end of the Long Island Sound as well as on Martha's Vineyard.

The Lawrence Pottery is included in the history of yellow ware, not because it produced yellow ware but because it acted as a wholesaler for the ware well into the 1900s. It should be noted that in the northeast many pottery companies producing stone ware and redware acted as agents for the wholesaling of yellow ware. This adds confusion as to who actually made yellow ware and who did not.

MAINE

One company producing yellow ware in Maine is worth noting, and that is the Bangor Stoneware Company, 1880. The company was large and produced a line of yellow ware, as seen in the 1886-1887 *Maine State Yearbook and Legislative Manual*, which stated that the company not only dealt with stone ware and fancy pressed ware but also in Rockingham and yellow ware. The clay was imported, it is believed by schooner, from New Jersey and Great Neck, Long Island.

CONNECTICUT

Entering Connecticut, the focus for yellow ware must be turned to Norwalk, which has a magnificent early history in redware and stoneware. From 1825-1835, the community thrived with potters producing wonderful redware, slipware and stoneware. The second half of the century saw the descendants of Asa Smith run a most successful pottery. Two companies seem to have dealt with yellow ware in Norwalk.

Learning the pottery trade in New Jersey, Absalom Day came to Norwalk to ply his trade in 1793. He and his wife worked the factory until 1831 when they willed it to two of their sons: Noah S. and George Day. It is under these two

Extremely rare yellow ware cow pitcher. Found normally with a Rockingham glaze. This pitcher measures 5⅜" high at head and 6½" in length. Bennington Museum Collection, Vermont.

men that the production of yellow ware and Rockingham began, but it was very short-lived. There is some speculation that yellow clay was used before this venture, but not to be presented in the form of yellow ware. Under Day's sons, yellow ware was definitely made, since an advertisement read "Three or four apprentices to the Earthenware and Yellow ware business..."[4].

As the Day family dominated much of the pottery world of Norwalk in the early part of the century, the Smith family dominated the pottery trade in the second half of the nineteenth century. They did not, however, produce yellow ware at Norwalk. The yellow ware often attributed to this company was sold out of their New York warehouse, made to the company specifications either at the Swan Hill Pottery in South Amboy, New Jersey or in East Liverpool.[5]

Produced for sale by the company were jelly moulds with wheat, corn and grapes, chamberpots with one or two handles, and footwarmers in two shapes: slanted and shaped like isosceles triangles or tunnel-shaped with a flat bottom, and a half-circle top with a cork in the side.

The knowledge that this company did not produce its own yellow ware gives further evidence of the scarcity of this product in the northeast. The tunnel-shaped footwarmer also belies the often-heard reference that these footwarmers were made in Europe. This company had an extensive history, stretching from 1812-1890, and traded under four names: Smith and Day, A. E. Smith and Sons, A. E. Smith's Son's Pottery Company and finally the Norwalk Pottery Company

NEW YORK
Touted as a major yellow ware producing area, New York did produce massive quantities of stoneware, but its yellow ware proclivity remains unknown to this author. Three areas seem to have produced some yellow ware, but the thrust of New York's pottery efforts lie in the stoneware field. Major areas of yellow ware production seem to be

Footwarmer originally believed to be of English origin due to shape, but known to have been made in New York State.

Syracuse, Utica and Poughkeepsie. Makers of this utilitarian ware in the Syracuse area were the W. H. Farrar and Company, 1857-68, Charles Manchester and Fischer W. Clark 1868-9, Thomas G. White 1869-?, and the Syracuse Stoneware Company, which produced yellow ware in the 1890s, as seen in an 1896 catalogue. The company, among other things, produced banded white and brown chamber pots and nested mixing bowls.

In the Utica area, the White Pottery Company, steeped in wonderful stoneware history, may have made a line of yellow ware. No hard evidence has been found, however, to determine whether they produced or just sold yellow ware.

Although reputed in the past to be a major yellow ware center, Poughkeepsie yellow ware potters remain somewhat elusive, with only two surfacing. These may even be wishful thinking. The first is the Caire Pottery Company, 1840-96. No history of yellow ware production, however,

has been found to date. But in a photograph depicting the wares manufactured by this firm, two yellow ware moulds are present. The second company is the Oncutt and Thompson Company, 1860-70. Again, there is no hard-core evidence that yellow ware was produced here. They did produce a Rockingham pitcher which would lead one to believe that perhaps they did produce some yellow ware for utilitarian purposes. The mark found on Oncutt wares reads "ONCUTT AND THOMPSON/ POKEEPSIE."

Before leaving New York, mention must be made of James Carr of New Jersey. After leaving The Swan Hill Pottery, Carr established a pottery in New York City with the aid of a Mr. Smith in 1856. By the following year, another partner by the name of Morrison was brought into the firm. The business was short-lived, with the main thrust of production being porcelains and Rockingham. At this time, there is no firm evidence that yellow ware was in production.

Pipkin with vertical rib design, pinched nose pourer, curved side handle measuring 6¼" high. Lid displays button-type finial. Note that pipkins may also be found with straight, hollow handles. Bennington Museum Collection, Vermont.

Large milk pan 12" in diameter and 4" in depth, displaying flared sides and semi-bulbous lip. Marked with the circular Lyman, Fenton mark. c. 1849. Bennington Museum Collection, Vermont.

Bucketbench collection of moulds including large, mini, and mini-mini moulds. Most moulds were produced in graduated sizes from New Jersey to Ohio.

Octagonal yellow ware preserve jar with screw-on top. Rare in this form produced in both New York and Ohio.

Mini-mini moulds are a late entry on the yellow ware scene. Some marked "Yellow Rose/Philadelphia" with a green or blue stamp under the glaze.

PENNSYLVANIA

Philadelphia reigned as pottery and porcelain king in Pennsylvania during the nineteenth century, possibly for the same reasons Trenton reigned supreme in New Jersey. Material was abundant; transportation, good; and the population clamoured for goods.

John Mullowny of Philadelphia formed The Washington Pottery in 1809, and could be viewed as a forerunner for the manufacturing of yellow ware. It is not clear whether he produced any yellow ware, but he did manufacture yellow pottery of a sort until 1816. Ware produced by Mullowny consisted of coffee pots, tea pots and pitchers.

The type of pottery Mullowny actually made cannot be documented except by an ad which described his wares as red, yellow and black coffee pots, tea pots and pitchers.

An important figure in the ceramic field in Philadelphia was Thomas Haig, who was born in England and trained as a queensware potter. He made two moves before purchasing land on the West side of Fourth Street above Poplar. There he built a pottery and worked it until his death in 1831. It must be believed that his sons James and Thomas took over the firm and began to produce yellow ware and Rockingham, including a Rockingham pitcher with a full relief of George Washington as a master mason. By 1842 the Philadelphia census listed James Haig as an independent potter and showed that he purchased a second pottery on Fourth Street. One pottery produced the stoneware and the other was set up for earthenware production. This company remained in business until 1890.

Andrew Miller started his pottery in 1785, and by the end of the century was producing both plain and decorated redware in abundance. By the turn of the century his two sons, Andrew Jr. and Abraham, had learned the trade, and by 1809 struck out on their own in a partnership that lasted until Andrew's death in 1824. By 1827 Abraham had bought out his sisters' share of the company for $4,660[6] and began to amass an empire, producing yellow ware, Rockingham, stove pipe and cooking stoves. In 1840 Miller moved his pottery to James Street, and it became known as Spring Garden Pottery. This pottery ran until 1851, when Miller expanded to Callowhill Street. The business was exceedingly successful, as can be seen by an ad in the Philadelphia Directory of 1857 which stated "...Where are manufactured and constantly for sale, or made to order, Portable, Dentist, and Culinary Furnaces, Stove Cylinders, Fire Brick and slabs; first quality Black glazed Tea Pots; common Earthenware, superior do viz-white, yellow and Rockingham ware... made promptly to order, in any quantity."[7] It has been stated in the past that after Miller's death, the company was run by the foreman, but this is unlikely; the plant was closed down in 1859-1860.

Beach or "Beech", as sometimes written, worked for Miller until 1845, then established his own pottery in 1848, producing both yellow ware and Rockingham. It is believed that he bought with him a Daniel O'Connell pitcher mould

which originally came from the Doulton Factory in England. These pitchers, which depicted the Irish patriot were made in both yellow ware and Rockingham in graduated sizes. The company closed its doors in 1851.

Philadelphia can not be left without a brief discussion of the J. E. Jeffords Company. Jeffords built a factory in Philadelphia in 1868 for the production of Rockingham. He had with him as chief designer Stephen Theiss of Bennington. His output was mostly in the realm of toby pitchers and cow pitchers. Although ceramic historians such as Ramsey limit his production to Rockingham, pitchers, yellow ware paneled bowls with stick sponge decorations and mugs have been attributed to him. Additionally, during the Philadelphia Centennial Exposition of 1876, the J. E. Jeffords, Philadelphia City Pottery was awarded a medal for its yellow ware exhibit.

Jeffords continued his pottery works, but soon began the production of white wares as the industry began to change in the late 1870s.

OTHER POTTERS

JABEZ VODREY 1827 East Liberties,
(Vodrey discussed in Ohio)
THOMAS ELVERSON 1862-80 New Brighton
PHOENIXVILLE POTTERY 1867-79
GEORGE A. WAGNER 1875-96

MARYLAND

Maryland has a history of scattered yellow ware potters, but the one most prominent in its production was the Edwin Bennett Company. Bennett established a pottery in Baltimore in 1846 after leaving his brothers in East Liverpool, Ohio. He began his company with the manufacturing of Rockingham and yellow ware. In 1848 his brother William joined his firm and the trademark "E.W. Bennett, Canton Street, Baltimore, Md." was established. After eight years of partnership, William left the firm and the trade mark was changed to "E.B." rather than "E.W." The company flourished well into the twentieth century, but by 1870 the pottery began to produce white ware. Some of the best pieces of Rockingham were produced here by Charles Coxon, a master modeler who presented the firm with Rebecca at the Well, hound-handle pitchers and a standing stork pitcher. Most of these items were copied all over the country by Rockingham producers.

Coxon proved that unless marked, yellow ware is difficult if not impossible to identify, for potters and modelers took their ideas and forms from one company to another, producing similar wares. As pictured on page 34, these mugs are attributed to Coxon. However, one was produced in New Jersey, probably while Coxon worked for Swan Hill, and the other was produced in Maryland for Bennett. Without the Bennett mark, this piece could mistakenly be attributed to New Jersey.

INDIANA

Four companies come to light in Indiana as follows:

INDIANA POTTERY 1837-38
JABEZ VODREY 1839-47
JAMES SAUNDERS AND SAMUEL WILSON 1851-63
BENJAMIN HINCHCO 1865-88

Yellow ware was produced at the Indiana Pottery from its onset in 1837 under the direction of James Clews, the noted Staffordshire potter. He came to Troy, Indiana from Kentucky, and established a pottery. Although a brilliant potter in England working with soft paste historical blue and white, he was a complete disaster in America. Within the year he was out of business due to unskilled workers and the use of inferior clay. Replacing him was Vodrey. After the original Clews factory burned down, John Saunders and Samuel Wilson took over, continuing to produce yellow ware and Rockingham. This partnership was followed by Benjamin Hinchco, who continued the same line of production.

Yellow ware potteries, although predominent in the states that have already been discussed, did by no means limit themselves to these areas. Potteries cropped up in the nineteenth century and well into the twentieth wherever transporation lines and raw materials were made easily available. Kentucky housed the Lewis Pottery Company as early as 1829 with Clews, Vodrey, and Frost plying their hands at the business of producing white ware. Failing in this, they turned to the manufacture of yellow ware in such commodities as pie plates, cuspidors and soap dishes.

Delaware saw such potters as Abner Marshall producing yellow ware from 1860-1866; and even in Kaolin, Missouri Elihu H. Shepert and George Pyatt, of Zanesville fame, tried to produce this utilitarian ware from 1853-1863. Fenton of Bennington struck out to Peoria, Illinois and produced yellow ware there in 1859. It would seem that this seldom-thought of ware was quite important in the nineteenth century, for as far west as Wisconsin and California, yellow ware was produced to meet the needs of the people. Two California firms tried producing yellow ware. One, in Elsinore, California, later moved to Riverside, trading under the name "Pacific Clay Manufacturing Company". The other was J. A. Bauer and Company of Los Angeles.

Yellow ware ruled supreme between 1840 and 1870, as evidenced by contemporary potteries dotting the country. At this point in time, perhaps just the surface has been scratched as to the number of companies that produced yellow ware. Surely this is just the beginning, but like anything else one must start somewhere, and fill in the blanks with new information.

With New Jersey and Ohio leading the way, the role of yellow ware should at this point be firmly implanted in the history of pottery in the United States. It served as a transitional and experimental ware that took our industry out of the primitive and the use of redware, into the modern with white ware and porcelains still to come. Through the histories outlined in these chapters it is time to dispense with the notion that yellow ware was a mere whim. The need for a transitional ware existed, and hundreds of potters served it well. On the way they developed the techniques and knowledge to lead us into the modern era.

CHAPTER 6

HINTS

Yellow ware collecting today can almost be considered in its infancy. Time after time a would-be collector or a novice will ask "how do I begin?" or "what makes a good collection?" From these conversations arise basic questions that should be answered before a collection is amassed.

1. What forms are available?
2. What pieces are rare?
3. What age are these pieces?
4. What condition is acceptable to collect?
5. What price should be paid?
6. Where should I look for yellow ware?

This chapter will endeavor to answer these questions. As with any rule, there are always exceptions, and there are times when instinct should rule the mind. That is where the fun comes in.

Common pieces to collect include: mixing bowls, milk pans, nappies, pie plates, mugs, some moulds, custards, plain and pressed bowls, chamber pots, butter pots, bedpans, lipped bowls and covered dishes or bowls.

Less common pieces to collect include: scalloped nappies, oval and rectangular bakers, rectangular serving plates, wash bowls, mini moulds, mini crocks and jugs, mini or toy chambers, soap drainers, pitchers, rundlets, footwarmers and spittoons.

Rare items are those not seen commonly at shows or in shops. As yellow ware becomes more highly sought-after, however, many of these items will change categories because they will begin to surface in the market place. Some of these items most desirable to the collector are: washboards, meat tenderizers, mini cups and saucers, preserve jars, rolling pins, lustre-decorated pie plates, stick or cut sponge-decorated yellow ware, pipkins, flower pots, animal and human moulds, dinner plates, baskets, snuff boxes, bird baths, pepper pots, master salts, colanders, figural matchsafes, mustard pots, coffee pots, cow creamers and inkwells.

Any of the above items becomes more valuable with applied decorations of Rockingham, mocha or sponge. It is a matter of taste as to whether or not to collect these wares.

1. Common mixing bowls—One of the most common of all forms collected, may be plain or banded, with one band or numerous bandings in white slip, greens, bricks, grays, and browns or mocha. Banding may be narrow or wide.

White, narrow bands tend to be the oldest form of decoration on yellow ware. The bowls may be collected as a single unit or in nests. Note that although frequently seen in nests of 5, most bowls were manufactured in nests of 8 to 12. The bowls likely to be missing are the smallest, which is 4″ in size, or the bowls over 9 inches. The largest nested bowls are usually 17″. Prices will vary with size, the smallest and largest at times may be the most expensive because of scarcity. Mixing bowls were made throughout New Jersey, New England, Ohio, New York and Maryland. When collecting mixing bowls, condition should be mint, large bowls over 10″, however, may have minor damage and still be desirable.

C. 1840-1930. Average price $20-$200 depending on size.

2. Milk pan—Mostly made in plain yellow ware and Rockingham, can be collected in nests of 4 or 5 sizes, and are often mixed up with nappies. Milk pans seem to have a turned lip, where nappies are flared with no lips. Milk pans were made in all areas that manufactured yellow ware. Age can be told by the three stilt marks or imperfections seen in the glaze on the bottom of the pan. These marks were created by a glaze-drying process. Condition of milk pans should be good to mint. Some wear on the bottom is passable but no cracks or minor flakes are acceptable. An interesting note is that some milk pans display pads or feet on the underside in the form of hearts, clovers, diamonds and rectangles. These different bottoms are a collection in themselves.

C. 1850-1880. Average price $60-$125.

3. Nappies—Usually found in plain yellow ware in 6 to 9 sizes from 4″ to 12″. This bowl type is often confused with milk pans. These dishes are round, deep and flared on the sides with no turned lips. They can be found in abundance; and the largest sizes are more desirable and more expensive. Nappies were produced in most areas. Condition should be near-mint.

C. 1840-1900. Average price $40-$100 depending on size.

4. Pie plates—One of the most common forms found in yellow ware, these plates make wonderful pies. Usually found in 4 or 5 sizes, with early examples hand-thrown and displaying stilt marks. Condition should be near-mint. Some crazing and burnt glaze on bottom is acceptable due to the function of the piece. Cracks and chips, however, should be avoided. Over 10″ pie plates are hard to find and

Late line of yellow ware bowls, heavy in composition with thick lips. Front 2 pieces display pressings. Bowl on left signed "Roseville".

Display of medium-sized bowls demonstrating semi-flared lip, semi-rolled lip, and straight lip.

Nest of 5 yellow ware bowls. Demonstrating semi-rounded lips and impressed band around bottom. As discussed in text, may have originally had up to 12 graduated sizes to complete the nest. Diameters here 6", 7", 8", 9", 10".

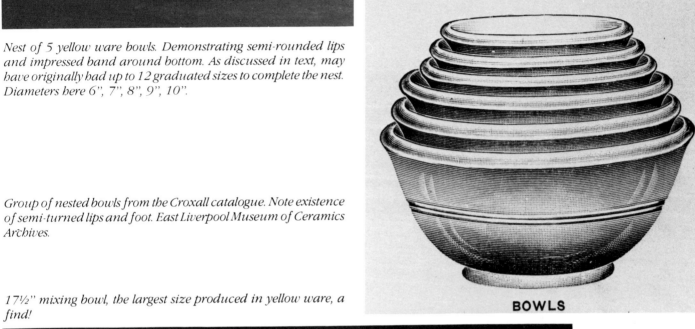

36s, 30s, 24s.

Group of nested bowls from the Croxall catalogue. Note existence of semi-turned lips and foot. East Liverpool Museum of Ceramics Archives.

BOWLS

17½" mixing bowl, the largest size produced in yellow ware, a find!

NAPPIE DISHES

Nest of nappies advertised for sale. Note flared, straight sides and no lips. East Liverpool Museum of Ceramics Archives.

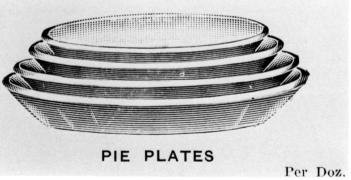

PIE PLATES

Per Doz.

Nest of pie plates from Croxall catalogue. East Liverpool Museum of Ceramics Archives.

Nest of pie plates, early examples of yellow ware. Smallest and largest plates (over 10") hard to find on market today. Diameters 7¼", 8¼", 8¾", 9¼", 10", 11", and 12".

36s

12s

Plain mugs with applied handles seen in Croxall price catalogue. East Liverpool Museum of Ceramics Archives.

should be obtained when seen with condition used as a variable.
C. 1840-1890. Average price $60-$125.

5. Mugs—Found more and more on the market today, mugs usually have an applied handle and come in 1 to 3 sizes. They may be decorated with slip bands 1 or more or mocha bands in seaweed. The forms taken may be straight or flared sides, wide or narrow bodied. Many of the mocha-banded mugs were imported from Canada, where yellow ware is called cane ware, and the mocha design is called dipped ware. England, too, was a major exporter of mocha-banded mugs. In the United States these mugs were produced in Ohio and New Jersey. Condition of mugs should be good with no chips. Mugs may display some minor flaking if mocha-banded.
C. 1860-1930. Average price $80-$250.

6. Moulds—Called jelly or corn moulds, are a late addition to yellow ware. They are usually found in three forms, oval, hexagonal or round. Early moulds were round with cone-shaped interiors in a swirl pattern. These were copied from the European turks head moulds. Most of the common moulds have a fluted impressed interior. The most common display corn, wheat or grapes on the bottom of the moulds. Some moulds have been found with maker's signatures; for example the I. W. Cory mould of Trenton, New Jersey. Animal and human form moulds are out there but considered rare, as are some mini moulds. The corn and wheat moulds came in at least 3 sizes, and should be collected as such. Condition of common moulds should be good, with impressed forms completely visible. Some crazing and discoloration is acceptable. Flakes and chips should not be accepted on wheat, corn and grape moulds, for there are too many still available.
C. 1860-1930. Average price common: $100-$150.

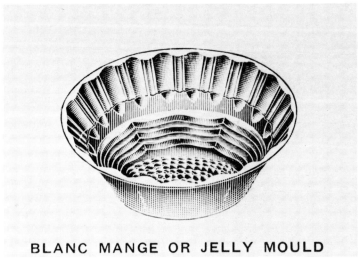

BLANC MANGE OR JELLY MOULD

Typical corn mould, called Blanc Mange *or jelly mould in the 1890s. These moulds were produced from Vermont to New York, and across to Ohio. East Liverpool Museum of Ceramics Archives.*

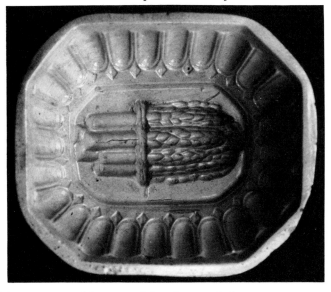

Asparagus mould unusual in clarity of design and subject. Shown in octagonal form. Height 3¼", length 7¼", width 6¼".

CUSTARD CUPS

Typical nested custards produced throughout yellow ware history. East Liverpool Museum of Ceramics Archives.

Grouping of custards, common in the yellow ware market but a collection unto themselves due to the variety of styles and sizes produced.

7. Custards—Small and cup-like in appearance, custards were originally cone-shaped. Later they displayed bands, and still later were moulded and impressed with geometric figures. These designed custards are less common but available. Condition of custards should be mint, for they were not only a late entry in the yellow ware market but are still easily found in the marketplace.
C. 1870-1930. Average price $25-$50.

8. Pressed bowls—These bowls may be banded or plain with embossing and pressing evident in geometric and scenic designs. These are usually quite heavy with semi-turned rims. May be footed or not. These bowls are very common and tend to take the shapes of ironstone bowls. They are made in graduated sizes, usually 8 to a nest. Although very common at the turn of the century or later, these bowls were produced much earlier than previously thought. Condition when buying should be mint and the collector should establish a nest of each pattern.
C. 1865-1930. Average price $25-$70.

Mocha-banded yellow ware in seaweed pattern produced in England and the United States. Mug demonstrates an applied handle.

Collection of mugs produced in the United States and England. All demonstrate applied handles and numerous banding decorations.

Assortment of common corn moulds. All 3 demonstrating different shapes. Can be collected in graduated sizes.

Yellow ware chamber pot. Impressed vertical design with applied handle displaying a semi-flared lip.

CHAMBERS

Chamber pots with mocha seaweed application, produced lidded and unlidded. East Liverpool Museum of Ceramics Archives.

French bedpan, one of two styles produced in Ohio. East Liverpool Museum of Ceramics Archives.

9. Chamber pots—Common and somewhat undesirable as a collectors' piece, however, should be added to a rounded yellow ware collection. Found in plain yellow, pressed, or mocha-banded and Rockingham motif. Chambers were sold both lidded and unlidded with applied handles. Three or four sizes available. Condition should be mint. They make great flower pots!
C. 1840-1890's. Average price $45-$150 depending on banding.

10. Bedpans—Done in plain yellow and Rockingham. By the nature of its being, hardly collected and therefore not expensive at all.
C. 1860-1890. Average price $25-$45.

11. Butter pots—Found mostly with bands, ranging in color from white, green, brick, gray, brown and black. They usually come in 4 sizes from 1 quart to 1 gallon. Lids have same banding as pot and display low, button-shaped finials. These pots are highly collectible and are often used as cannister sets. Some pots have the word "butter" on the white slip bands. Lids are interchangeable, but the collector must be careful in matching lid bands with pot bands if bought separately. Butter pots are hardly ever found in mint condition; most display chips on rims of lids or hairline cracks in pots due to use. Often will also display flaking on bands. Minimal damage accepted, pots without lids also acceptable.
C. 1860's-1890's. Average price $60-$125.

12. Lipped bowls—These are often given the name "batter bowls" due to configuration of their pinched pouring spouts. Found in plain, banded and impressed geometric designs, they can be found in 4 sizes.
C. 1860-1900. Average price $75-$150.

13. Covered bowls—These are squat or low compared to mixing bowls, and were originally sold with covers. They were a late production model for yellow ware and resemble modern casseroles. Can be found plain or banded, especially with white and brown bands. Used primarily for storage or serving. Condition should be good.
C. 1870-1920. Average price $50-$60.

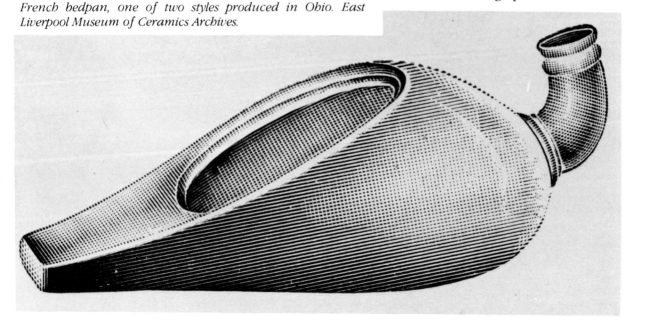

*Collection of covered butter pots or crocks, forerunners of yellow
ware cannister sets. Stamped "Butter" on piece. Diameter 6½",
height with cover 5". Lid diameter 7½".*

*Butter pots demonstrating gray and white banding. Note sick slip,
often found on butter pots and other mocha-banded ware.*

Lipped bowl with fluted design, often referred to as a batter bowl.
Can be found in graduated sizes. Diameter 14", height 6½".

LESS COMMON

1. Scalloped nappies and rice dishes—Mostly plain yellow with vertical rib impressions to appear scalloped. These are usually found in six sizes. Can be confused at times with low bowls, but look more like nappies. Difficult to find on the East Coast. Condition should be good, some minor hairlines acceptable since these pieces are hard to find.
C. 1860-1900. Average price $60-$125.
2. Oval and rectangular bakers—These are multi-purpose dishes, used for both serving and baking. Not found easily because of the use they received in kitchens. Can be found in 7 sizes, from 6" to 12", and can be nested. Condition should not be important in a purchase decision, for most of these bakers show signs of wear, on the bottoms some have burn marks, others have scratches inside from being used as serving pieces. Most desirable to collect in nesting forms, but it is difficult to find all sizes. Both oval and rectangular have semi-flared sides and may show semi-rolled lips. Over 10" size most difficult to find.
C. 1860-1900. Average price $75-$150 depending on size.
3. Rectangular serving plates—All yellow, no decorations, found seldom, but available if sought. These plates predominantly made in New Jersey and Ohio. Some have been signed such as "Henderson, Jersey City". Early design somehow lost as yellow ware matured into the late 1800s.

Early plates extremely shallow and heavy-bodied. Condition not important, for these are early pieces and may show great wear. Should be purchased when found.
C. 1830-1870. Average price $100-$200.
4. Wash bowls—Found mostly in plain yellow, perhaps should be considered rare. Known to have been produced in Ohio by the Phoenix Pottery Works of East Liverpool in 1865-6. Washbowls came in 2 sizes, 11" and 12", and sold in 1865 for $2.00 and $2.75 respectively per dozen. May now be at times confused with large mixing bowls.
C. 1860-?. Average price $85-$175.
5. Mini moulds—produced by many companies and are collections in themselves. Most common are wheat and corn in round, oval and hexagonal form. Can also be found in fruit, grapes, and asparagus designs. Mini-mini moulds are a late entry into the world of yellow ware and took the forms of hearts, diamonds and melons. Some of these moulds are signed with "Yellow Rose/ Philadelphia" stamped under the glaze. This company at present remains an enigma but would seem to be a late manufacturer of yellow ware. Moulds may be called jelly moulds or *Blanc Mange* moulds in some areas. Condition should be fair to good and may display minor flakes and chips. However, enough of these are coming onto the market that mint condition moulds are available. When purchasing, design on bottom of mould should be clear and recognizable.

BAKERS—OVAL

Nest of 7 oval bakers, not easily found today. These bakers demonstrate a semi-rounded lip. Wonderful to bake in. East Liverpool Museum of Ceramics Archives.

C. 1870-1930. Average price $18-$95 depending on design.

6. Mini crocks, jugs, and pitchers—Usually 1" to 2" in height and may have green or Rockingham glazes applied. Made early in the late 1840s in Bennington, Vermont and were produced West to Ohio by the 1870s. Made as novelty pieces or toys, jugs and pitchers have applied handles and crocks display elephant ears. These mini pieces are valuable in most conditions. At times they are overlooked and can be bought much under true value.

C. 1850-1875. Average price $50-$150.

7. Mini chambers—Pure novelty and advertising gimmicks, these mini chambers can be found in numerous sizes with flat lips or semi-rounded. Can be collected in plain yellow; banded, especially white and brown; or with advertising printed on the bands. An example of this is a white-banded mini chamber which reads, "Mist of the Maid 1896". In itself a rarity, for it should have read "Maid of the Mist". These make a charming small collection and range in size from 1½" to 3". Condition should be good; many are available.

C. 1880-1900. Average price $45-$75.

8. Soap drainers—Unusual to be found in yellow ware, most common form is Rockingham. Mostly found New Jersey, New York and some in Ohio. Condition should be good but not necessarily mint, for many flakes and chips found on undersides.

C. 1860-1890. Average price $45-$65.

Nest of oval bakers, unusual to find today.

SQUARE NAPPIES.

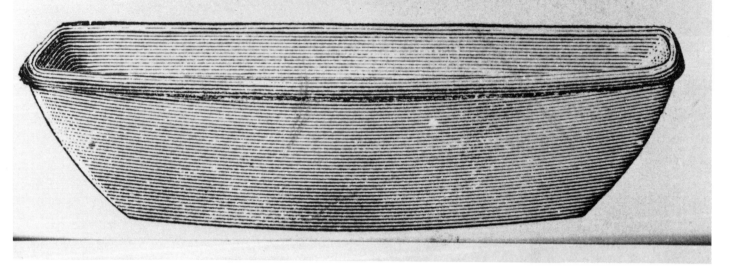

Square nappies, unusual to find today. East Liverpool Museum of Ceramics Archives.

YELLOW WARE

TOY CHAMBERS

Advertisement showing toy chamber, produced as novelty pieces by many yellow ware companies. East Liverpool Museum of Ceramics Archives.

Classic pitcher, bulbous form, pinch nose spout and applied handle. Three-area banding indicative of classic style.

9. Pitchers—Found in plain yellow, banded or mocha-banded. These were small, almost creamer-sized, and termed in most advertisements as "Turned Pitchers". Made in 4 sizes from 1 pint to 3 quarts. These make wonderful collections themselves, should definitely be sought in graduated sizes. They can be found plain or impressed, and have applied handles. Considered rare are larger pitchers with impressed decoration, such as the hound-handle pitchers produced in New Jersey, Vermont, Maryland and Ohio. These pitchers are found mostly in Rockingham but were sparingly made in yellow ware. If found, they should be added to a collection no matter what the condition. Condition of plain pitchers should be good, exhibiting handles intact and no chips or hairlines in pouring spout.
C. 1835-1900. Average price $75-$225 plain and banded, $1,000-$2,500 hound-handle or decorated.

10. Rundlets—Somewhat rare, these are usually found in plain yellow, shaped like kegs. May demonstrate a flat or rounded back, flat being the rarer of the two. These were found in different sizes up to 3 pints. Can be found thrown or moulded, and were used to hold water or liquor. Found only sparingly now, were not likely to have been popular at their inception because they were somewhat fragile and clumsy to handle. Condition may vary, accept with hairlines and chips because of scarcity on the market.
C. 1860-1900. Average price $80-$150.

11. Footwarmers—Found in plain yellow, originally thought only wedge-shaped was American but America also produced a round or tunnel-shaped footwarmer with a flat bottom. New York, New Jersey and Ohio show some production of this ware. Hole plugged with a cork, as of yet no ceramic tops have been found. Still available and may be bought under-value, for footwarmers are not considered desirable pieces. However, a must to a complete collection. Condition should be good, minor corner chips acceptable.
C. 1860-1880. Average price $115-$250.

Collection of 3 pitchers demonstrating size, style, and color differences exhibited in yellow ware. Left front piece showing splotches of Rockingham glaze.

Mini chamber collection produced throughout yellow ware areas as novelty, toy and advertising pieces. Found banded, plain, mocha-banded and inscribed.

12. Spittoons—Most commonly found in Rockingham and can be seen plain and in an octagonal or round form, at times impressed with shells. Rare in plain yellow ware and even rarer if found embossed with a floral decoration in each divided panel. Somehow neglected as a collectors item, but when seen in plain yellow ware should be purchased. Minor chips and flakes off edges acceptable. Spittoons can be frequently found off-price because of their present desirability.
C. 1850-1900. Average price $50-$100.

Rare items are those not seen commonly at shows or in shops, as yellow ware becomes more highly sought-after, however, many of these items will change categories. Somehow more and more will surface, for it is the nature of the beast!

1. Washboards—Wonderful pieces to collect, not listed in many catalogues and can be found in plain yellow, Rockingham and a yellow ware with blue glaze applied. Blue and yellow at this time would seem to be the rarest form, as Rockingham washboards can be found more easily. These pieces are found largely in Ohio and the New England states. Condition of yellow ware can be flaked or chipped, but board around slab of yellow ware should be in good condition and firmly supporting yellow slab. Important piece to add to any collection, and still available at a price.
C. 1860-1800. Average price $350-$500.

2. Meat tenderizers—Extremely rare, found mostly in Ohio, and have eluded most price catalogues from yellow ware companies. Would assume this to be a late entry into the yellow ware market and one that was short-lived. Not many found today, not only because of time frame in which it was produced but because of the nature of its use seeming to be self-destructive. Condition no concern, if found add to your collection.
C. 1870-1890. Average price $150-$250.

Wedge-shaped footwarmer, one of two shapes produced in the United States. Prevalent throughout the northeastern production area.

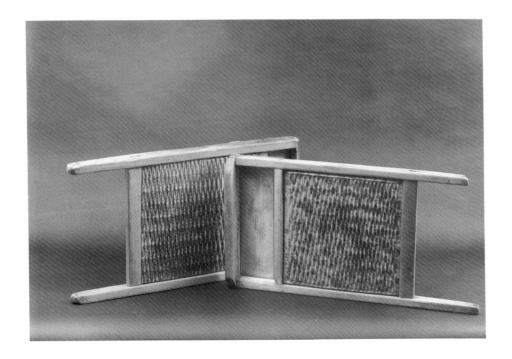

Washboards demonstrating a yellow ware with a blue glaze and a Rockingham glaze. Predominantly found in the Ohio area. A must to a complete collection. Plain yellow is the rarest found.

Yellow ware with applied Rockingham glaze demitasse cup and saucer, unusual piece to find.

Preserve jars showing 3 different styles. Front piece demonstrating screw on top.

3. Mini cups and saucers—Found to be a Vermont novelty, referred to as toy cups and saucers. These items measure 2″ for a saucer and 1″ high for cups. Handles are applied and pieces are rather crude in form. These cups and saucers can be found plain, Rockingham-glazed and green sponge-glazed. Most minis are highly desirable for any collection. Condition unimportant, may display minor flakes or chips on rims and under saucers. Handles should be in good condition.
C. 1850-?. Average price $100-$150.

4. Preserve jars—Found in plain yellow in four closure forms, screw on ceramic tops, cloth wax sealers, tin wax sealers and gum sealers. Forms found are usually round or hexagonal, but the Phoenix Pottery Works of East Liverpool did advertise a barrel-shaped fruit jar with a yellow ware funnel in 1865. These are rare and should be purchased when seen whether tops are available or not. Ceramic-top fruit jars will display internal ridges in neck piece and wax sealers will have a wax well around the neck. They were manufactured in large numbers in Ohio. Due to the advent of glass, however, their popularity was short lived. Condition does not matter, for they are hardly ever found in mint condition because of the nature of use. Most common damage seen around the rims. May be purchased under-price especially at flea markets; because of rarity may be passed over as just another ceramic container.
C. 1850-1870's. Average price $75-$150.

5. Rolling pins—Although rare at this time and costly, it would seem that more and more are surfacing, and prices should get lower with time. Made in plain yellow with wooden handles. Important to the collector that handles remain firmly attached and that rolling action remain evident. Condition of pins at this time not very important, chips and hairlines around edges acceptable.
C. 1870-1900's. Average price $225-$425.

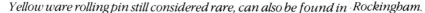

Yellow ware rolling pin still considered rare, can also be found in Rockingham.

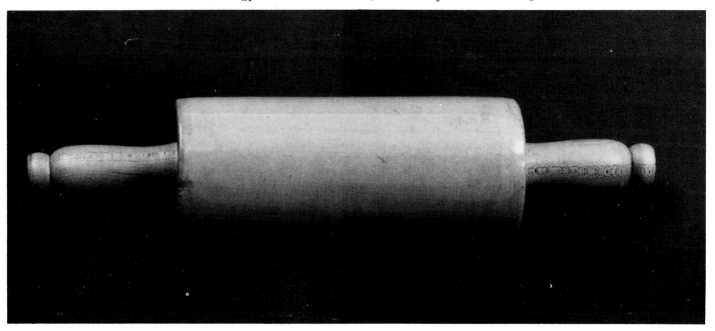

6. Lustre-decorated pie plates—Rare in existence, produced in New Jersey and possibly Pennsylvania. The art of lustre application came to America with some of the potters who began production of yellow ware in the United States. It would seem that the Trenton and Philadelphia area, which leaned toward the production of porcelains, created some of this lustre decoration on yellow ware. Pieces can be found in Tree of Life pattern as well as bird patterns, and should be considered part of American folk art. Would seem to have been an early endeavor that was short-lived due to expertise and expense of production. Stilt marks made from glazing process often found on these pieces indicating early production. These pieces can also be purchased underpriced because of their non-exposure. This author has recently purchased a Tree of Life lustre pie plate in pink lustre for $65, the going price for a good pie plate and then has seen lustre pie plates for $400 some months later. Condition not important, although large cracks do detract from lustre design.
C. 1840-?. Average price $300-$500.

7. Stick sponge decorated yellow ware—Found on small bowls out of the Philadelphia area as well as Trenton, New Jersey where large nappies were decorated. Known as cut sponge or stick sponge decoration, this design application has been attributed to the English children of the nineteenth century who would apply decoration with a potato stamp. Highly sought-after pieces, they should be added to any collection. Decorated pieces are a collection unto themselves, and are the fun pieces of yellow ware.
C. 1850-1870. Average price $100-$500.

8. Pipkins—Rare in any form, a wonderful word to describe a "Yankee" bean pot. Pioneer ingenuity reigns with this form. Most made as rounded pots with long hollow handles coming out of the side of the pot. The handle was hollow to allow steam to leave cooking vessel. Other pipkins can be found with curved applied handles. Lids are often no longer available. They can be found both plain and impressed mostly in Vermont; one is currently on display at the Bennington Museum. A must for the serious collector. Condition not important. Lids not a must. Chips and hairlines especially in handle acceptable. Although the production period was quite long, due to the use of the pipkin and the hollow handle, few have survived.
C. 1850-1890. Average price $175-$275.

9. Flower pots—Mostly found in redware or terra cotta, yellow ware flower pots are rare. Not popular as a collector's item yet, but should be added to a growing collection. Often the underplate of a flower pot mistaken for a small plate. Look for angular form rather than rounded. Flower pots were put out in Ohio by the Goodwin Pottery as early as 1850.
C. 1850-?. Average price $50.

10. Animal or Human Form Moulds—Boars, rabbits, lions, deer, and human forms such as fishermen are extremely rare in the mould world and should be sought. Unlike common moulds, these seem to take on the shape of the impressed figure rather that maintaining the conventional round, hexagonal or oval form. Condition not primary, at times difficult to see impression in piece, but once identified should be added to a serious collection. Found throughout yellow ware areas.
C. 1860-1900. Average price $100-$300.

11. Dinner plates—Considered rare, may be found in plain yellow with crude body, tending to be quite heavy and embossed. Some found slightly lighter in body, displaying embossed scenic designs around edges of plates. These plates have been found both round and hexagonal. Rarely seen advertised, they were definitely produced by the C. C. Thompson and Company, East Liverpool, Ohio, in 4 sizes. Condition not important.
C. 1880-1900. Average price $85-$125.

12. Baskets—Novelty items of yellow ware, tend to be heavy and crude in form. Moulded in one piece most times. Found largely in Ohio and Pennsylvania. An oddity to add to a collection, not often seen. Can't be too choosy about condition.
C. 1870-1920. Average price $85-$125.

13. Birdbaths—Extremely rare, have seen none to date. Ohio main source of production as early as 1865. As of yet no value assigned, but what a find if one is obtained.

14. Pepper pots—Known also as master peppers, these pepper containers demonstrate large holes on the top, usually have cork plugs if any available. Often found with mocha bands in seaweed or worm pattern. These were imported from Canada and England as late as the 1920s. The pepper pots are approximately 3" high. They are rarely seen in plain yellow. Condition rarely mint, usually exhibit some chips and flakes especially around bottoms or around the mocha banding. A must for a great collection! Average price $200.

15. Master salts—These, like the pepper pots, are often found with mocha bands in seaweed or wormy patterns. Most are open salts and footed. Rarely found and a must for any serious collector. May have been imported from Canada, and definitely from England.
C. 1850-? Average price $225-$275.

16. Colanders—Widely collected, may be plain yellow, yellow-banded, mocha-banded or yellow with a white interior. Designs of holes may be random, clustered circles or star patterns and may have holes on the bottom half of colander or all over. Basically two types, most commonly found in a round form but can also be found straight-sided. Colanders are highly sought-after and at times scarce, however, more and more are appearing, and will probably surface in greater numbers as demand heightens. Note: until recently white interiors were thought to be European; this is not true. Ohio produced a white interior colander. Other yellow ware from Ohio also demonstrate white interior in mugs, bowls and pitcher sets.
C. 1870-1900. Average price $200-$325.

Most unusual boar mould exhibiting museum quality.

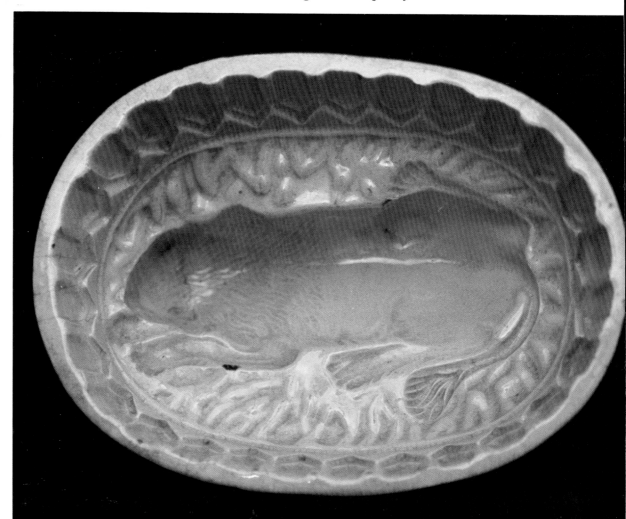

Rare oval lion mould. Height 4¼", length 8½" and width 6¼".

Pair of luncheon plates, impressed design around edges displaying Western scene. It would seem from form, design and composition that these pieces were made in England for the American market.

Decorative novelty pieces. Yellow ware baskets are crude in form. Most found with impressed designs.

Novelty pieces produced throughout the 1880s and 1890s. Piece on the left is one of a series of matchsafes. On right is a doctor's bag with removable top.

17. Figural matchsafes—Basically found in plain yellow in both crude and refined forms. A would-be Victorian notion, some demonstrate snowflake body effect. Usually in the form of buildings, people and animals. At this time origins unknown, although found in both Ohio and New York, with the Syracuse Pottery Company putting out figural political mugs in the 1920s. Some question must arise concerning the nature of these pieces and their age. Would seem to be late because of their Victorian nature. Some examples are signed with a BB or DD on the bottom, either signifying potters' mark or mould mark or piece identification. All the facts not in on figurals but should be added to any collection.

C. 1880-1930. Average price $75-$225.

TURNED JUGS

Colander exhibiting white interior. Until recently thought to be an English import but known to have been made in the United States. Holes presented in a star pattern in lower half of colander. Other patterns and random holes also produced. Diameter 10", height 5".

Turned jugs, or what we call milk pitchers, mocha-banded with seaweed design. East Liverpool Museum of Ceramics Archives.

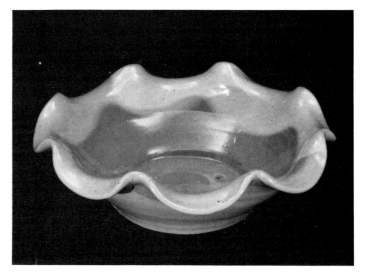

Fluted serving or vegetable dish, unusual for its style. Considered rare.

Soap dish rare in plain yellow ware, most commonly found in Rockingham. This piece is attributed to Knowles, Taylor & Knowles. East Liverpool Museum of Ceramics Collection, Ohio.

Yellow ware stag matchsafe with snow overglaze. From detail and design would lend itself to an English origin.

Small mustard, a wonderful piece, displaying a pewter top and applied handle. These mustards are also found with ceramic lids and bandings.

18. Mustards—Found in plain yellow with pewter or tin tops, and ceramic yellow ware tops. Lids must match in banded-ware, and make sure it is a mustard top with spoon hole before buying.
C. 1870-1920. Average price $150-$250.
19. Coffee pots—Exceedingly rare and usually very ornate. Most seen now in museums, and their form tends to copy European styles. Earliest pieces made in New Jersey by Henderson at the Jersey City Pottery circa 1830. These pieces remain exceedingly rare because they were made early and discontinued by the 1860s.
C. 1835-1860. Average price $400-$1500.
20. Cow creamers—Known better with a Rockingham glaze applied to the yellow ware, rare in plain yellow. These creamers were made in the early 1850s at Bennington Vermont, and were produced at the United States Pottery Company. The cow creamer, because of its novel look, was also made in Ohio and New Jersey. Condition not a major drawback in purchase. A must for the serious collector.
C. 1850-1880. Average price $300-$600.
21. Inkwells—Rarely found in catalogues but definitely produced in Ohio and Vermont. Usually found in figural forms such as animals, specifically dogs. A must for the advanced collection. Inkwells have been found in Ohio with a blue glaze decoration over yellow ware.
C. 1860-1900. Average price $200-$300.

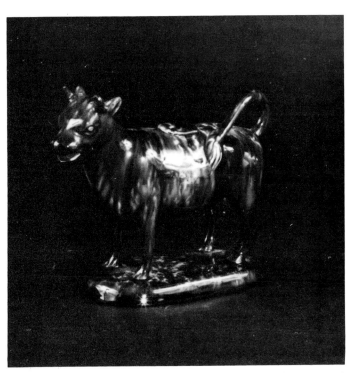

Rockingham cow pitcher, popular in England and the United States. Important piece to any collection, extremely rare when found in plain yellow ware.

Fisherman's mould, a rare piece that should be added to any collection.

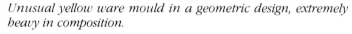

Unusual yellow ware mould in a geometric design, extremely heavy in composition.

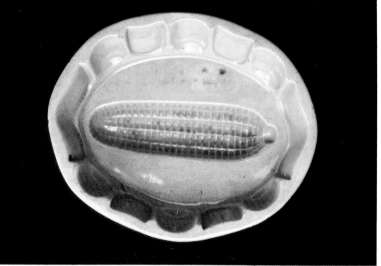

Individual corn mould, unusual in fluted design and clarity of corn impression.

96

This chapter has discussed basically American forms or similar forms found in production in America, Canada and England. For further information on truly English forms refer to the chapter on England in this book. The differences discussed will help the collector to further identify yellow ware pieces.

Once knowing what to look for and approximate value, the next question is where to look. Three places seem most helpful in this endeavor: the flea market, the auction house and the antique dealer. Stories of great finds continue to come from all three areas, although tales are known to get taller with repetition.

Flea markets, marvels in themselves, may be very helpful, but the collector must know exactly what he is looking for and have a good knowledge of price before he ventures forth looking for his find. It is at the flea markets that the best bargains are usually gained. Even the commonest of pieces may be priced at half of their value, and the rare pieces are at times overlooked due to lack of identification. The flea market offers many treats, but buyer beware; know your field before investing here.

Auctions are another marketplace for yellow ware. Surprisingly, yellow ware is often ignored by the auctioneer, but this, I am sure, is a temporary situation. At present, however, the fact holds, and auctions may be your best bet for collecting. I once obtained a beautiful little mustard pot with white-slip bands in a box lot I paid $20 for, and a pie plate with heart shaped feet for $5. Bowls and nappies can easily be found at most auctions. One auction, recognizing what they had, advertised yellow ware preserve jars. At auction time they sold two different shapes individually for $85 each and then lotted the remaining four, which were sold for $50 each. A real bargain!

When buying at auction, get there early, and make sure to see every piece you intend to bid on. Often the auctioneer will not call damages on minor pieces they sell on the theory "as is, where is". The second thing to remember when buying at auction is to set a price that you are willing to pay and stick to it within a limited range. Often one can be caught up in "auction fever" and find that much desired $100 piece is worth $50.

The most reliable source for amassing a collection, however, is the antique dealer. Dealer sources are unlimited, and their buying network can stretch all over the country. Pick a knowledgeable dealer who has a collection of yellow ware on hand and discuss the formation of a collection, or the pieces you are interested in purchasing. You may pay a bit more, but you'll get what you want as far as condition and rarity. Most dealers will be only too glad to work with a collector. The key here is the word "knowledgeable"! It is always unfortunate when a piece turns out to be 1920 when you asked for an early item. When buying, ask why and how. A good dealer will enjoy discussing the history of a piece and if he doesn't have an answer he'll endeavor to find it.

Twentieth-century pieces have not been discussed in this book, aside from English companies producing yellow ware into the 1920s which still exhibited a Victorian flair. At present, these pieces cannot be correctly termed antiques. The collector may enjoy adding these pieces to his collection, but should keep in mind that currently the prices these pieces are commanding are not merited. Often, as yellow ware production declined potters would try to put out a cheap ware by combining odd, leftover clays and glazing them yellow or brown. This is generally what twentieth century yellow ware is. A mystery clay of sorts, almost like prime ribs on the third night! Many of these pieces are very heavy, with thick lips and a stoneware feel.

By the 1920s Roseville came out with a type of yellow ware with a paper label. The mixing bowls are buff-colored, with white slip bands. By the 1930s, Weller was putting out their Reno pattern a dark, almost mustard, yellow with a brown band. During this time U.S.A. wares and "oven-proof-ware" also were introduced. Roseville and Weller are collectible and may be added to your collection as late examples, but U.S.A. and ovenproof-ware should be at this time avoided as collector pieces. A nest of early yellow ware bowls can be purchased for $125-$250. Yet these newer pieces, bountiful on the market place, are commanding almost as much. Buyer, beware.

With this information, the collector is ready to face the world of yellow ware. Be objective and liberal of mind once out in the market, for this is just the beginning of understanding yellow ware, not an end-all. Look for the odd pieces, the different designs and forms; they're out there to be discovered and catalogued. Yellow ware information as well as collecting remains in its infancy, but the more we look for it, the faster and stronger the field will grow!

Oval vegetable dish, deep yellow in color.

Yellow ware decorative pieces done with snow overglaze. Definitely a Victorian influence.

Rockingham-glazed yellow ware piggy bank popular during the 1880s. Unusual to be found in plain yellow ware.

Yellow ware butter churn with 2 top inserts. A rare find in yellow ware.

CHAPTER 7

ENGLAND

Believed to have been produced in England from the late eighteenth century through the early twentieth century, the history of yellow ware in England has proven no less difficult to trace than in the United States. Once again, this common ware eluded many historians and present-day curators, and has been steeped in confusion basically due to nomenclature.

Correspondence with many museum curators and ceramic historians concerning the question "did you produce a yellow-bodied clay with a clear alkaline glaze?" has yielded various answers. Some felt that no such ware was produced with a clear alkaline glaze in the Staffordshire district; and they were right. Others termed the ware I was looking for "yellow glazed earthenware". We know this term is not correct. Still others thought it could possibly be called a lead-glazed banded ware that was produced in England from the late 1700s through the 1800s. A Mr. Smith confirmed that through archeological digs in the "out-potteries" he has found a "yellow ware" that he would be shortly writing about. All of the correspondence only led further to the belief that yellow ware was in England, but terminology was the key problem in identifying this ceramic form.

The answer to the terminology gridlock came from correspondence with Geoffrey Godden, noted British ceramic historian, writer and dealer of antiques. He wrote in reference to this problem, "Indeed much, if not all, of the trouble is in terminology. However, we certainly used the term 'Yellow Ware' but little or nothing has been written up about these utilitarian wares".[1] Mr. Godden unlocked the doors to English yellow ware, supplying some potters' names and the advice to consult Jewitt's *The Ceramic Art Of Great Britain*, 1878 or 1883 edition. The search was on.

Before potters are discussed, a few broad facts should be presented about English yellow ware. Most of the potters who migrated to America to produce yellow ware were from the Staffordshire district of England. It must be noted, however, that this district did not produce yellow ware as we know it. The yellow ware of England, although scattered throughout the northern and western portion of the country, came basically from the Derbyshire area or more specifically the Woodville area of Derbyshire. This leads to the terminology problem, for from Jewitt one

Rare English individual hunt tureen done in a basketweave pattern on underplate and tureen with heavily impressed game scene on cover. This tureen also displays a buff-colored insert.

Master opened salt. English in design.

Victorian matchsafe believed to be English in origin. Detail work exceptional for yellow ware.

learns that most of this utilitarian ware was called not only yellow ware, but also Derbyshire Ironstone Cane Ware. In discussing the Swadlincote Potteries, Jewitt described yellow ware as "...Derbyshire Ironstone Cane (or yellow) Ware" (a name by which this ware has for upwards of a century been known, and which is the specialty of the district);..."[2] The reason for its production would seem to be that it was inexpensive to produce, available in great quantities in some areas, could resist heat and was inexpensive to the consumer. Another fact that must be addressed is that Scotland also had a hold on the manufacture of yellow ware.

It would seem that unlike the production process of yellow ware in the United States, where one finds potters migrating across the country as well as clay being shipped north and south to produce yellow ware, English potteries were more home-based, tending to be cottage industries. The wares produced would seem to have been based on the clays found in the immediate areas of production. Perhaps that is why not much has been recorded or known of the production of yellow ware.

Another fact is that production of yellow ware in England did not begin much before the production of yellow ware in the United State. In broad terms, perhaps England began manufacturing some 30 to 40 years before America did. Along these lines still another fact comes to light, that of longevity. England, as did the United States, produced this ware well into the twentieth century. But unlike the United States, where form was changed to a more modern deco look, England maintained traditional forms and Victorian styles in her production of this ceramic ware.

Before discussing form differences between American and English goods, it would be best to give the collector an idea of the time frame and location of those potteries in England and Scotland that produced yellow ware. Information is scant at this time, and the list is not complete, but what is known must be entered as a beginning in the search for potters and their production lines.

Yellow ware production, it would seem, began at the Swinton Rockingham Works in Yorkshire, England. Swinton, known throughout the world for its production of Rockingham, also dabbled with yellow ware. Unlike American Rockingham, which has a yellow base, Jewitt describes the Rockingham of Swinton as a white ware. "This Rockingham ware, which was of a fine reddish-brown or chocolate color... The body was of fine hard and compact white earthenware...[3] Established in 1778 by Thomas Bingley, and originally called Thomas Bingley Company, Swinton went on to produce some of the greatest Rockingham the world has ever seen, including toby figures called the "Snuff Takers", which have been copied all over England.

The next pottery to produce yellow ware opened its doors in Glasgow, Scotland in 1780, and remained in business until 1928. Originally established by Reed, Patterson and Company and called Glasgow Pottery, by 1807 it was in the hands of Actchison and Company and renamed Caledonian Pottery. By 1870 it was moved from Glasgow to Rutherglen, where it continued to produce Rockingham.

The first pottery in the Derbyshire district known to have produced yellow ware was the Swadlincote Pottery, which was established in 1790 by John Hunt. Known for the production of yellow ware and sewage pipe, the firm stopped production of yellow ware around 1880 and turned to the manufacture of sanitary ware.

Between 1790 and 1820, many potteries came into being producing yellow ware, amongst other earthenwares. One of the longest track records was held by the Church Gresley Pottery in Derbyshire. This firm ran from 1790 well into the twentieth century. It was established by a Mr. Leedham, who produced utilitarian wares, and then sold to W. Bourne. Mr. Bourne began the production of yellow ware, naming it Derbyshire Cane Ware. Before 1864, the company was taken over once again, but for the sake of yellow ware, our interest begins with T. G. Green and his purchase of the firm in 1864. It is here that yellow ware and Rockingham flourished. The company expanded its production, and as late as 1926 was producing three types of yellow ware: plain yellow, white interiors and mocha-decorated.

From a circa 1926 T. G. Green and Company Ltd. catalogue we learn that the production line of yellow ware was vast. In white interiors, Green produced round and oval casseroles in four sizes, round stew pots, cake pans, round and oval nappies in fourteen sizes from 1″ to 14″, hot pots, bakers, starch pans, brawn pans with handles, pressed colanders, lipped nappies and milk pans in 7 and 6 sizes respectively, and lipped and round bowls.

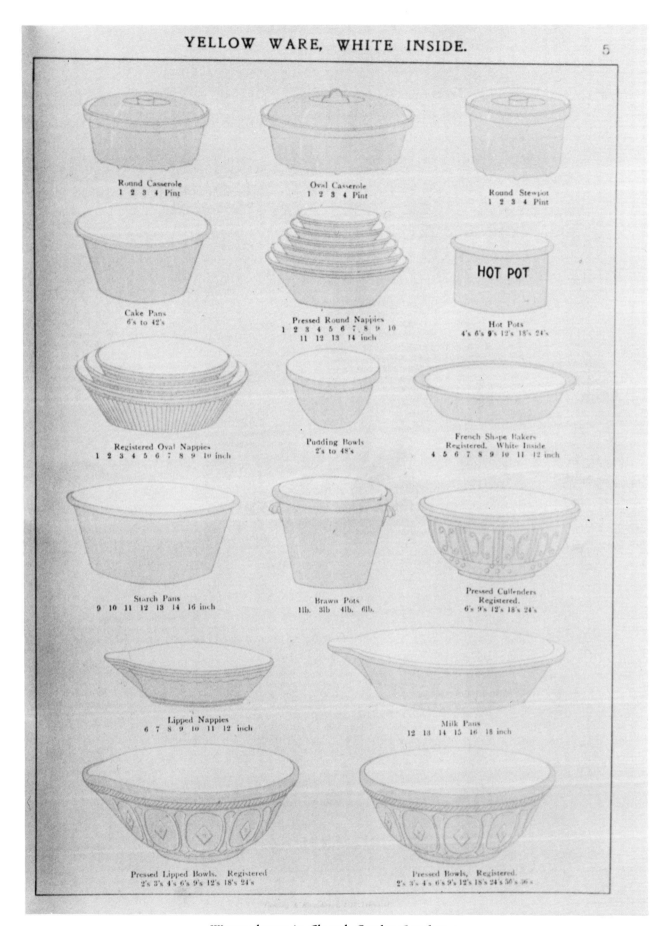

Round Casserole
1 2 3 4 Pint

Oval Casserole
1 2 3 4 Pint

Round Stewpot
1 2 3 4 Pint

Cake Pans
6's to 42's

Pressed Round Nappies
1 2 3 4 5 6 7 8 9 10
11 12 13 14 inch

HOT POT

Hot Pots
4's 6's 9's 12's 18's 24's

Registered Oval Nappies
1 2 3 4 5 6 7 8 9 10 inch

Pudding Bowls
2's to 48's

French Shape Bakers
Registered. White Inside
4 5 6 7 8 9 10 11 12 inch

Starch Pans
9 10 11 12 13 14 16 inch

Brawn Pots
1lb. 3lb. 4lb. 6lb.

Pressed Cullenders
Registered.
6's 9's 12's 18's 24's

Lipped Nappies
6 7 8 9 10 11 12 inch

Milk Pans
12 13 14 15 16 18 inch

Pressed Lipped Bowls. Registered
2's 3's 4's 6's 9's 12's 18's 24's

Pressed Bowls, Registered.
2's 3's 4's 6's 9's 12's 18's 24's 30's 36's

Wares shown in Church Gresley Catalogue.

Ship Shape Jugs
2's to 36's

Covered Butters
9's 12's 18's 24's

Yellow Covered Jars
2's to 24's

Ship Shape Jugs
2's to 36's

Pear Shape Jugs
2's to 36's

Porter Mugs
12's to 36's

Covered Ship Jugs
White Band

Ship Shape Jugs
Plain Yellow

Porringers
18's 24's 30's

Porter Mugs
White Band
12's to 36's

Covered Sugars
18's 24's 36's

Common Bowls
2's to 48's

Pudding Bowls, Yellow
4's to 48's

Covered Mugs
White Band
12's to 36's

Covered Bowls
White Band
5's to 36's

Hot Pot Basins
18's 24's 30's 36's

Rice Jars
2's to 24's

Hand Basins, Yellow
3's 4's 6's 9's 12's

Brown Top Jars
2's to 36's

Round Rim Chambers
4's 6's 9's 12's 18's 24's

Covered Chambers
4's 6's 9's 12's 18's 24's

Flat Rim Chambers
4's 6's 9's 12's 18's 24's

Stone Household Jars
4's 6's 9's 12's 18's

Footwarmers

Stone Pudding Bowl
2's to 48's

Wares shown in Church Gresley Catalogue.

102

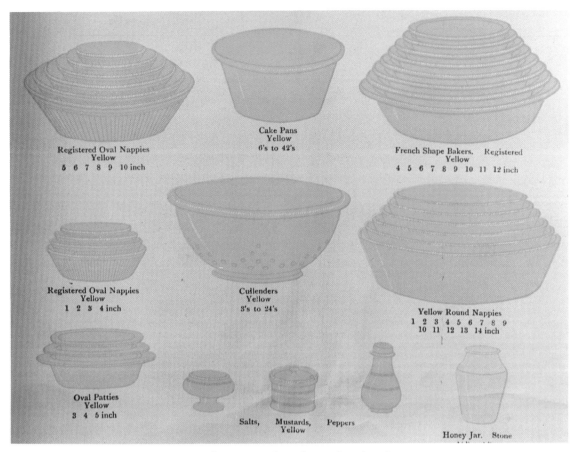

Registered Oval Nappies
Yellow
5 6 7 8 9 10 inch

Cake Pans
Yellow
6's to 42's

French Shape Bakers.   Registered
Yellow
4 5 6 7 8 9 10 11 12 inch

Registered Oval Nappies
Yellow
1 2 3 4 inch

Cullenders
Yellow
3's to 24's

Yellow Round Nappies
1 2 3 4 5 6 7 8 9
10 11 12 13 14 inch

Oval Patties
Yellow
3 4 5 inch

Salts,   Mustards,   Peppers
Yellow

Honey Jar.   Stone

Wares shown in Church Gresley Catalogue.

In decorated yellow ware with mocha and seaweed bands, the firm produced ship shape mugs and jugs, pear-shaped jugs with mocha and seaweed, covered butters in four sizes, covered jars, covered mugs, covered sugars in three sizes, footed bowls, porringers in three sizes with mocha-seaweed bands, covered bowls with white and mocha bands, hot raisin basins in four sizes, covered rice jars, hand basins, covered and uncovered chambers, and flat, rimmed chambers in multi-seaweed patterns in six sizes.

In plain yellow ware they produced oval nappies in 5 sizes, round nappies in fourteen sizes from 1″ to 14″, colanders, oval patties in three sizes, salts, peppers and mustards.

Much of the Church Gresley yellow ware is marked with a stamped circle in black under the glaze showing a picture with a church beneath which is inscribed "Gresley Church". The mark may also display, "Made in England and Mfg.#."

In Scotland the Alloa Pottery was formed in 1790. The company remained in existence until 1908. During the first two ownerships yellow ware was not manufactured. It was not until 1855, when the company came into the hands of W. and J. A. Bailey, that the production of yellow ware commenced. Known basically for its production of majolica and Rockingham, yellow ware was merely an addendum to round out their production line. It has been stated that so much Rockingham came from this pottery by 1870 "...twenty-six thousand teapots could be produced by them per week..."[4] It is also believed that this was the first company to manufacture majolica in Scotland.

1790 saw yet another pottery form in the Derbyshire district. This pottery has a vague history of producing yellow ware and was named the Hartshorne Pottery. It remained in existence until 1895.

From the early 1800s through 1820, ten potteries appear on the landscape of both England and Scotland all producing yellow ware. Early in the century in Fremington, North Devon, a company by the name of The Pottery was set up by George Fishley, and was passed on from son to son until 1912. Known for the production of fire-brick ovens, the company also produced yellow ware and redware from local clays. From 1800c. to 1880c. the Leeds Pottery of Yorkshire, although resoundingly noted for their cream ware or "Queensware", had a half-hearted fling with yellow ware. It would seem that to begin with the company was producing fine cream wares, but by the 1870s the firm turned half of its production to utilitarian wares, one of which was common yellow ware. The Leathley Lane Pottery in Leeds also produced a line of yellow ware and Rockingham from the turn of the century until 1890. For this production they used the clays found in Worthley.

Yellow ware with white interior mixing bowl. English in origin and signed "Church Gresley".

English mocha-banded container. Typical of mocha banding with brown decoration bleeding into the white slip.

During the same time frame the Rock Pottery or the Mexbro' Pottery in Mexborough, Yorkshire came into existence. Jewitt believes that it was established to produce brown and yellow wares by Mssrs. Ford and Beevers. It would seem that this company produced household goods such as dishes and mugs. By 1839 finer forms of pottery were being produced by James. The company closed its doors in 1883.

In 1802 the Belle Vue Pottery Company came into existence in Yorkshire. It did not receive the name "Belle Vue" until 1826 when it was taken over by William Bell from the Ridgeways. In production until 1840, the company under Bell produced a yellow ware butter pot in the shape of a cow.

The Derbyshire district saw two potteries open in 1810: the Hill Top Works owned by John Copper, which remained in existence well past the turn of the century; and the Woodville Potteries, which had a history from 1810-1895 under the direction at first of Watts and Cash. Both firms produced yellow ware for utilitarian use. Some pieces from the Woodville Potteries were marked with an impressed "WOODVILLE POTTERIES".

The Waterloo Pottery was established in Derbyshire in 1815 by Robinson and Rowley, but had numerous owners, ending with R. C. Staley who owned the company twice. By circa 1891 the company was out of business, but had a record of producing both yellow ware and Rockingham. Three years later, still in Derbyshire, Joseph Thompson opened the Hartshorne Potteries to produce yellow ware. This company remained in business until 1882, with some of its pieces marked "J. Thompson" or at times, "Joseph Thompson/ Wooden Box/ Pottery/ Derbyshire".

By 1817, the Wooden Box Pottery in Derbyshire was established. Believed to have received its name due to the wooden toll booth that previously sat on the site of the pottery, this company produced yellow ware under the direction of Thomas Nadim until 1900. Some pieces were marked with an impressed "WOODEN BOX."

In Sinclairtown, Scotland the Fife Pottery or the Gallatown Pottery was established circa 1820 for the production of earthenware, one of which was yellow ware. The main thrust of this company, however, was the famous Wemyss ware which is a white earthenware.

By 1821, Thomas Sharpe had established the Sharpe, Brothers and Company or the Swadlincote Potteries. The main thrust here was Derbyshire Ironstone or yellow ware. From a 1891 catalogue, one learns that they produced a fine line of yellow ware and Rockingham, including teapots, impressed bowls and flat-lipped vegetable bowls. By 1895 the company turned to the production of sanitary ware.

From 1825-1856 the Shipley Company in Derbyshire was in existence producing, among other earthenwares, yellow ware. By 1856 the company was incorporated with the Denby Pottery under the direction of Bourne. Still in Derbyshire, the Woodville Pottery was shortly established in 1833. This pottery should not be confused with the Woodville Potteries of earlier note. This company pro-

ducing yellow ware remained in existence well into the twentieth century under the direction of Thomas Betteridge. Some pieces from Woodville have been found with an impressed "WOODVILLE POTTERY" mark.

The Coleorton Pottery c. 1835 and the Rawden Pottery c. 1840 were the next two companies to produce yellow ware in Derbyshire. Coleorton remained in existence until 1895; and Rawden under the direction of T. C. Dooley closed its doors in 1986. Both produced a line of yellow ware and the Rawden Pottery marked its pieces with an impressed "RAWDEN POTTERY" mark.

In Yorkshire in 1864 the Denaby Pottery was established. Prior to producing yellow ware, this company had been a fire-brick factory. John Wardle and William Wilkinson took the company over in 1864, and although yellow ware was not the main commodity of the company, it did produce this utilitarian ware for a short period of time.

Edward Grice established the next pottery to produce yellow ware. As of this time, no starting date has been found, but it is known that by 1873 the firm known as the Commonside Pottery in Derbyshire was taken over by Mason, Gaugh and Till. Shortly, Mason left the company, and it continued producing yellow ware until 1895.

In Scotland, two other potteries must be mentioned. The first is Bayley, Murray and Brammer, who established the Saracen Pottery in 1875 and ran it into the twentieth century. Here mostly utilitarian wares were produced for export. Some Saracen pieces have the mark "BM & Co. Saracen Pottery" impressed in the piece. In the same year, the Rosslyn Pottery in Fifeshire was opened. This company was known to have made piggy banks and other barnyard figures in Rockingham. By 1883 the company expanded to the production of both majolica and yellow ware.

William Mason, whom the reader has seen before, established the Pool Pottery in 1880, and produced an extensive line of yellow ware into the twentieth century. The last company to be discussed is the Old Midway Pottery in Derbyshire, which at this time has no dates established. It was founded by a Mr. Grange and taken over by Richard Staley. Under Staley's direction the firm produced yellow ware. Some pieces were signed "Richard Staley and Sons", and some pieces may exhibit the words "fire proof" after the name.

This compiled list of potters may be cursory. It does, however, establish the fact that yellow ware was not only produced in England, but also in Scotland. The list also allows the collector to establish time frames for pieces in their collections. What must also be understood is that some companies, such as Gresley Church, not only had offices in England, but also set up show rooms and offices in Canada. This leads to the problem of not only "is it American" but also "is it really Canadian or just imported from England". Due to the similarity of these wares, unless marked or of truly English form, identification is nearly impossible.

As discussed in Chapter 1, there are some differences in American and English yellow ware; however, white interiors should not be considered one. The density of clay

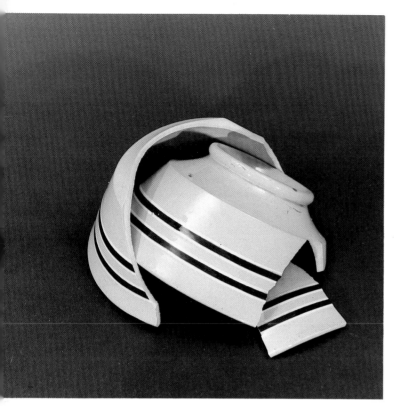

Chards of an English mocha-banded bowl demonstrating yellow straight through with a clear glaze application.

would seem to be one difference whereby English yellow ware in some forms seems finer than American. This density also lends itself to the theory that English pieces will ring when struck. This may be correct. As previously discussed, however, fine American pieces will ring also. What may prove to be helpful in some ways in distinguishing the two wares is to become familiar with the forms produced and the sizes manufactured by the two countries.

Just looking at the pages of the Church Gresley Catalogue supplied here will help the collector as to form. For example, the United States did not produce lidded mugs, brawn pots, or starch pans. What should also be noted is that lipped bowls in the form of nappies were rarely if at all produced in the United States. The same holds true the other way around. England did not produce pipkins, washboards or, it would seem, rundlets. So form may definitely be of service in identifying country of origin.

Sizes also may be a clue to origin or ware. For example the English produced nappies in 14 sizes form 1″ to 14″ while most of the American manufacturers produced 10 to 12 sizes none of which were as small as 1″ to 2″. Another point to digest is that many English chambers and some bowls had flat-rimmed lips rather than round or semi-rounded lips, as displayed on American types. That is not to say that all round-lipped bowls are American because England also produced these types.

Still another difference between the two is number of colors used in decoration. It would seem that England put out mocha-banded yellow ware in a seaweed pattern with three colors. This use of tri-colors does not appear to my knowledge in American mocha-banded yellow ware. Caution again should be taken, for although the English put out this tri-color mocha-banded ware, that is not to say they didn't put out a bi-color as did the United States.

Mugs in graduated sizes with applied handles, produced with thinner bodies. These mugs manufactured in England.

Yellow ware mug demonstrating multi-banded slip work, with intricately designed collar and applied handle. Detail work and fineness of composition would suggest an English origin.

Two English yellow ware pieces. Note lid on creamer, a definite sign of English design.

Covered mug, double-banded with matching lid, applied handles and impressed lines at the bottom. English in origin. Piece measures 3½" high and 3¾" diameter.

Banded yellow ware chamber pot demonstrating straight lip, an example of English workmanship.

107

Large yellow ware mocha-banded bowl with green seaweed design.

With great hesitation I now mention the word Canada. Many pieces on the market place today, especially on the East Coast, claim to be Canadian in origin. What is most frequently seen is mocha-banded mugs and chambers with green seaweed patterns. At this time only a refined crystal ball would know if these pieces are indeed Canadian or English. In fact pieces attributed to the Branfort Pottery are termed "produced in the English manner".

What can be established at this time is that Canada produced yellow ware; and that two major companies involved in its production were the Branfort Pottery and The Cap Rouge Pottery. Some examples of Canadian yellow ware are housed at the Royal Ontario Museum in Toronto although the collection is small. Evident from the museum are bowls with mocha seaweed bands and plain mocha white bands. Going further into Canadian yellow ware would require a book just on Canadian production, which is something for the near future.

For now, the collector must try to be content with the knowledge that this utilitarian ware was produced first in England, then in the United States and Canada. Marked pieces, although rare, are available, and this book will aid the collector in establishing yellow ware origins. Whether English, American or Candian, this book establishes the viability of this ware, and allows yellow ware to take its place in the world of ceramics as an authenticated transitional ware.

NOTES

Chapter 1: YOU COLLECT WHAT?

1. J. Jefferson Miller II, *English Yellow-Glazed Earthenware* (Washington: Smithsonian Institute Press, 1975), 4.
2. Miller, *English Yellow-Glazed Earthenware,* 5.
3. Rita S. Gottesman, comp., *The Arts and Crafts In New York, 1729-1776* (New York: N.Y. Historical Society, 1938), 90-1.
4. John Spargo, *Early American Pottery and China* (Vermont: Charles E. Tuttle Co., Inc., 1974), 196.
5. J. G. Stradling, "American Ceramics and the Philadelphia Centennial," *The Magazine Antiques,* July 1976, 155.

Chapter 3: NEW JERSEY

1. Margaret E. White, *Decorative Arts of Early New Jersey,* N.J. Historical Series, Vol. 25 (Princeton, N.J.: D. Van Nostrand Company, Inc., 1964), 40.
2. Lura, Woodside Watkins, "Henderson of Jersey City and His Pitchers," *Antiques,* December 1946, 389-90.
3. Archibald M. Maddock II, *The Polished Earth, A History of the Pottery Plumbing Fixture Industry in the United States* (Published by the Estate of Archibald M. Maddock II, 1962), 43.
4. Arthur W. Clement, *Our Pioneer Potters* (York, Pa.: Maple Press Co., 1947), 32-3.
5. White, *Decorative Arts,* 40.
6. Maddock, *The Polished Earth,* 52.
7. Maddock, *The Polished Earth,* 50.
8. *Early Arts of New Jersey The Potters Art c. 1600-1900,* an Exhibit at the New Jersey State Museum (Trenton, N.J.: Department of Education of N.J., 1956, Catalogue), 32.
9. Edwin Atlee Barber, *The Pottery and Porcelain of the United States* (New York: G.P. Putnam's Sons, 1893), 213.
10. Barber, *The Pottery and Porcelain of the United States,* 213.

Chapter 4: OHIO

1. William C. Gates Jr., and Dana E. Ormerod, *East Liverpool, Ohio, Pottery District Identification of Manufacturers and Marks,* Historical Archaeology Vol. 6, No. 1-2 (The Society for Historical Archaeology, 1982), 3.
2. William C. Gates, Jr., and Dana E. Ormerod, *East Liverpool,* 3.
3. William C. Gates, Jr., and Dana E. Ormerod, *East Liverpool,* 3.
4. William C. Gates, Jr., and Dana E. Ormerod, *East Liverpool,* 3.
5. William C. Gates, Jr., and Dana E. Ormerod, *East Liverpool,* 5.
6. "Centenary Anniversary of Harker Pottery Company" reprint, *The Bulletin of the American Ceramic Society,* Vol. 16, No. 1 (The Society for Historical Archaelogy, 1982), 3.
7. Lucille T. Cox, "The Story of John Goodwin, Pioneer Potter," *The Bulletin of the American Ceramic Society,* Vol. 21, No. 11 (November 15, 1942), 242.
8. Lucille T. Cox, "John Goodwin," 245.
9. Lucille T. Cox, "John Goodwin Finds a Woman's Place May Be in Her Husbands' Company' " *Potter's Herald,* April 1, 1937.
10. William H. Vodrey to Rhea Mansfield Knittle, May 2, 1938. East Liverpool Manuscript Collection.
11. Lucille T. Cox, "Isaac Watts Knowles," *American Ceramic Society Bulletin,* Vol. 21, No. 8 (August 15, 1942), 152.
12. William C. Gates, Jr. and Dana E. Ormerod, East Liverpool, 288.
13. William C. Gates, Jr. and Dana E. Ormerod, East Liverpool, 290.
14. Rhea Mansfield Knittle, "Muskingum County, Ohio, Pottery," *Antiques,* July 1924, 15-18.
15. Knittle, "Muskingum County, Ohio, Pottery," 17.
16. Paul Evans, *Art Pottery of the United States, an Encyclopedia of Producers and Their Marks* (Everybody's Press, Inc. 1974), 67.
17. John Spargo, *Early American Pottery and China,* 338, 9, 40, 41.

Chapter 5: ANCILLARY POTTERS

1. Lura Woodside Watkins, *Early New England Potters and Their Wares* (Harvard University Press, 1950; Archon Books, 1968), 212-213.
2. Lura Watkins, *Early New England Potters and Their Wares,* 90.
3. Lura Watkins, *Early New England Potters and Their Wares,* 88.
4. Lura Watkins, *Early New England Potters and Their Wares,* 201.
5. Andrew L. and Kate Barber Winton, *Norwalk Potteries* (New Hampshire: Phoenix Publishing, 1981), 132.
6. Susan H. Myers, *Handycraft to Industry Philadelphia Ceramics in the First Half of the Nineteenth Century* (City of Washington: Smithsonian Institution Press, 1980), 22.
7. Susan H. Myers, *Handycraft to Industry Philadelphia Ceramics in the First Half of the Nineteenth Century,* 74.

Chapter 7: ENGLAND

1. Geoffrey Godden, letter to Author, 17 January 1985.
2. Llewellynn Jewitt, F.S.A., *The Ceramic Art of Great Britain* (1883; reprint, Ward Lock Reprints, 1970), 375-6.
3. Geoffrey A. Godden, F.R.S.A., *Jewitt's Ceramic Art of Great Britain 1800-1900,* rev. ed. (New York: Arco Publishing Co., Inc., 1972), 231.
4. Geoffrey A. Godden, *Jewitt's Ceramic Art of Great Britain 1800-1900,* 147.

Time Lines

NEW JERSEY POTTERS

Jersey City	David Henderson (m)	· 1824-50	1824-28 Henderson, Dummer 1828-50 D. Henderson & J. Henderson "American Pottery Manu. Co."
Woodbridge	"Salamander Works" LeFoulon, Decasse (m)	· 1825-91	
South Amboy	John & William Hancock	· 1828-40	
Elizabeth	John Pruden Keen Pruden	· 1835-79	
Newark	Balthasar Krumeich	· 1836-c. 1900	
Newark	David Gillig	· 1840-c. 1900	1840-55 Gillig 1855-56 Gillig-Williams 1856-62 Gillig Osborne 1862-1900 Osborne & Sons
South Amboy	Abraham Cadmus "Congress Pottery" (m)	· 1849-61	1849-54 Cadmus 1857-60 Wooton 1860-61 William Allen
South Amboy	"Swan Hill Pottery" (m)	· 1849-76	1849-50 Sparks & Moore 1850 Hanks & Fish 1851 Cadmus 1852-55 Carr, Locker, Wooton 1857-60 Coxon 1860-71 John L. Rue 1871-75 Fish & E. O. Howell 1875-76 Perrine
Trenton	"International Pottery"	· 1853-c. 1857	Taylor, Speeler & Bloor
Trenton	Young, Millington, Astbury (m)	· 1853-57	
Trenton	William Young & Sons	· 1857-79	"Excelsior Pottery"
Trenton	"Carrol Street Pottery" (m)	·c. 1857-78	1857-59 Millington & Astbury 1859-78 Millington, Astbury and Poulson
Perth Amboy	"Eagle Pottery" W.H.P. Benton	· 1858-65	
Perth Amboy	Alfred Hall & Son	· 1866-87	
Trenton	I. W. Cory	· 1867-69	1868-69 Lawton
Union	"Union Pottery" Haide & Siph	· 1875	
Elizabeth	L. S. Beerbauer & Co.	· 1875	

OHIO POTTERS

Cinn.	James Doane	- c. 1831-37	
E.L.	James Bennett (m)	- c. 1840-44	
Musk.	Howson	- 1840-c. 1874	1840-46 Howson, Hallan, Wheaton c. 1846-63 Howson and Son 1863-74 John Howson
E.L.	Harker "Dynasty" (m)	- 1840-1972	1841 Tunnicliff & Whetton 1842 Tunnicliff, Goodwin, Croxall 1846-50 Harker, Taylor 1851-54 Harker, Creighton, Thomas 1854-64 George S. Harker, Thomas 1864-77 David Boyce 1877-1972 Harker Family
E.L.	Salt & Mear "Mansion Pottery (m)	- 1842-50	
E.L.	Goodwin Family (m)	- 1843-1913	1843 Goodwin, Tunicliff, Croxall 1843-53 "Eagle Pottery"—Goodwin 1863-65 "Novelty Pottery Works"—Goodwin 1872-75 "Broadway Pottery" John Goodwin and Sons 1875-93 Goodwin Brothers Pottery 1893-1913 Goodwin Pottery Co.
E.L.	Croxall Family (m)	- 1844-1910	1844-52 Thomas Croxall 1856-58 Croxall, Cartwright, Kinsey, "Union Pottery" 1858-88 Croxall, Cartwright 1888-98 J. W. Croxall & Sons 1898-1910 Croxall Pottery Co.
Cinn.	Kendall Family	- c. 1846-50	*may not have produced Yellowware
E.L.	Jabez Vodrey, Woodward Blakeley Co.	- 1847-1928	1847 Jabez Vodrey 1848 Vodrey, Woodward 1853-58 Vodrey, Woodward, J. & J. Blakely "Phoenix Pottery" 1858-96 Vodrey & Brothers Pottery "Palissy Works" 1896-1928 Vodrey Pottery Co.
Cinn.	Lessel Family	- 1848-99	1848-52 Peter Lessel 1852-79 Peter Lessel & Bro. 1879-99 George Lessel
E.L.	Brunt Companies	- 1848-1911	1848-53 Brunt & Bloor 1856-59 William Brunt & Bro. 1859-88 William Brunt Jr. & Co. "Phoenix Pottery" 1888-92 William Brunt & Son & Co. 1892-1911 William Brunt Pottery Co.
Musk.	Pyatt	- 1849-1900	1849-51 George Pyatt 1851-53 Pyatt, Getz 1866-79 George Pyatt 1879-1900 J. G. Pyatt "Tremont Pottery"
Cinn.	William Bromley "Brighton Pottery"	- 1849-?	1849-57 William Bromley 1857-60 Bromley & Joseph Bailey 1860-? William Bromley & Son
E.L.	Richard Harrison	- 1852-?	
Cinn.	George Scott	- 1853-1901	1853-89 George Scott 1889-1901 George Scott & Son
E.L.	Isaac Watts Knowles	- 1854-1929	1854-70 Knowles, Harvey "East Liverpool Pottery" 1870-1929 Knowles, Taylor, Knowles
Cinn.	Brewer & Tempest	- 1854-?	
Cinn.	Hamlet Greatbach	- 1854-56	
E.L.	"Salamander Pottery Works"	- 1855-86	1855-61 Flentke, G. & S. Morely, Godwin and Colclough

			1861-78 Morley, Godwin, Flentke
			1878-82 Godwin, Flentke
			1882-86 Flentke

Cinn.	Valentine Eichenlaub	- 1855-57	
Cinn.	Tunis Brewer	- 1856-59	
Cinn.	Henry Mappes	- 1857-?	1857-80 Henry Mappes 1880-? Henry Mappes & Brothers "Chester Park Pottery"
Cinn.	Andrew Behn	- 1857-77	
Cinn.	George Behr	- 1857-1900	
Cinn.	M & N Tempest	- 1859-65	
Cinn.	J. A. Brewer	- 1859-69	
Cinn.	Coultry Pottery	- 1859-83	1859-1870 Samuel Pollack "Dayton Street Pottery" 1870-74 Family 1874-83 Patrick Coultry
Cinn.	Tempest & Brockman Co.	- 1862-?	1862-81 Tempest, Brockman & Co. 1881-87 Tempest, Brockman & Sampson Pottery 1887-? Brockman Pottery Co.
E.L.	Agner & Gaston Co.	- 1863-?	1863-8 Agner & Gaston Co. 1868-? Agner & Foults
Musk.	Joseph Rambo	- 1863-c. 1870	
E.L.	Manley & Cartwright	- 1864-1927	1864-72 "Industrial Pottery Co." 1872-80 Manley, Cartwright & Co. 1880-96 Cartwright Bros. Pottery Co. 1896-1927 Cartwright Brothers Co.
Cinn.	Dallas Pottery- Fredrick Dallas	- 1865-82	
E.L.	C. C. Thompson Pottery Co.	- 1868-1932	1868-70 C. C. Thompson, J. T. Herbert 1870-89 C. C. Thompson & Co. 1889-1932 C. C. Thompson Pottery Co.
E.L.	McNicol, Burton Co.	- 1869-92	
Musk.	Alfred Wilber "North Ward Pottery"	- 1873-78	
Musk.	Calvin Bumbaugh "Star Pottery"	- 1873-1900	
Musk.	Duncan Hamelback	- c. 1874-80	
E.L.	"Star Pottery"	- 1875-88	Bulger & Worchester
Musk.	N. K. Smith	- 1878	
Musk.	Jacob S. King & John T. Swope	- 1879-1900	
E.L.	"Globe Pottery" (m)	- 1881-1912	1881-1901 Fredrick, Shenkle, Allen 1901-07 "East Liverpool Pottery Co." 1907-12 "Globe Pottery"
E.L.	John Patteson & Sons Pottery Co.	- 1883-1917	1883-1900 John Patterson & Sons Co. 1900-1917 Patterson Brothers Co.
E.L.	D. E. McNichol Pottery Co.	- 1892-1954	

ANCILLARY POTTERS

Conn.	Day Pottery	- 1793-1849	Yellowware began 1831
Conn.	Smith Pottery	- 1812-1890	Smith, Day A. E. Smith & Sons A. E. Smiths' Sons' Pottery Co. Norwalk Pottery Co.
Penn.	Jabez Vodrey	- 1827-c. 1830	
Penn.	Abraham Miller	- 1827-1860	
Penn.	James & Thomas Haig	- 1831-1890	
N.Y.	Claire Pottery	- 1840-96	
Vermont	Fenton (m)	- 1845-58	1845-47 Norton, Fenton 1849-58 Lyman, Fenton
Maryland	Edwin Bennett (m)	- 1846-1870	
Penn.	Beach	- 1848-51	
Mass.	Boston Earthenware Factory	- 1852-58	
Mass.	New England Pottery Co.	- 1854-75	
N.Y.	W. H. Farrar & Co.	- 1857-68	
N.Y.	Oncutt & Thompson	- 1860-70	
Penn.	Thomas Elverson	- 1862-80	
Penn.	Phoenixville Pottery	- 1867-79	
Penn.	J. E. Jeffords Co.	- 1868-70	Production of Yellowware
N.Y.	Charles Manchester & Fischer W. Clark	- 1868-69	
N.Y.	Thomas G. White	- 1869-?	
Penn.	George A. Wagner	- 1875-96	
Mass.	Boston Pottery Co.	- 1878-1900	
Mass.	Somerset Pottery	- c. 1880-1909	
N.Y.	Charles N. White	- 1886-1909	
N.Y.	Syracuse Stoneware	- c. 1890	
Maine	Bangor Stoneware	- c. 1890-1913	

BIBLIOGRAPHY

Atterbury, Paul. ed. *English Pottery & Porcelain A History Survey.* New York: Universe Books, 1978. A compilation of articles orginally seen in *Magazine Antiques.*

Barber, Edwin Atlee A.M., PH.D. *The Pottery and Porcelain of the United States an Historical Review of American Ceramic Art from the Earliest Times to the Present Day.* New York: G.P. Putnam's Sons, 1893.

Barret, R.C. *Bennington Pottery and Porcelain: A Guide to Identification.* New York: Crown Publishers, Inc., 1958.

Blacker, J.F. *Collecting Old English Pottery.* Toronto, Canada: Coles Publishing Company Limited, 1980.

Branin, M. Leylyn. *The Early Potters and Potteries of Maine. Middletown, Connecticut: Wesleyan University Press, 1978.*

Clement, Arthur W. *Our Pioneer Potters.* York, Pennsylvania: Maple Press Co., 1947.

Denker, Ellen and Bert. *The Warners Collector's Guide to North American Pottery and Porcelain.* Clinton, New Jersey: The Main Street Press, 1982.

Early Arts of New Jersey The Potter's Art C. 1600-1900. Trenton, New Jersey: State Museum Department of Education, an Exhibition Catalogue, 1956.

Evans, Paul. *Art Pottery of the United States: An Encyclopedia of Producers and their Marks.* New York: Charles Scribner's Sons, 1947.

Gates, William C. Jr. and Dana E. Ormerod, *East Liverpool, Ohio, Pottery District Identification of Manufacturers and Marks.* Historical Archaeology, 16 (1-2). The Society for Historical Archaeology, 1982.

Godden, Geoffrey A. *British Pottery and Porcelain 1780-1850.* U.S.A.: A.S. Barnes and Company, Inc., 1963.

_____, *Jewitt's Ceramic Art of Great Britain 1800-1900.* Revised Edition. New York: Arco Publishing Company, Inc., 1972.

_____, *British Pottery An Illustrated Guide.* New York: Clarkson N. Potter, Inc./Publisher, 1975.

Hughes, G. Bernard. *English and Scottish Earthenware 1660-1800.* London: Abby Fine Art.

Huxford, Sharon and Bob. *Collectors Encyclopedia of Roseville Pottery.* Kentucky: Collector Books, 1976.

_____, *Collectors Encyclopedia of Weller Pottery.* Kentucky: Collector Books, 1979.

Jewitt, L. *The Ceramic Art of Great Britain.* London: Virtue & Co., 1878 (revised 1883).

Ketchum, William C. *Early Potters and Potteries of New York State.* New York: Funk and Wagnalls, 1970.

_____, *Pottery and Porcelain.* New York: Alfred A. Knopf, 1983.

Lewis, Griselda. *The Collector's History of English Pottery.* New York: Viking Press, Inc., 1969.

Maddock, Archibald, M. II. *The Polished Earth, A History of the Pottery Plumbing Fixture Industry in the United States.* Estate of Archibald M. Maddock, II, 1962.

Miller, J. Jefferson, II. *English Yellow-Glazed Earthenware.* Washington, D.C.: Smithsonian Institution Press, 1975.

Myers, Susan H. *Handycraft to Industry: Philadelphia Ceramics in the First Half of the Nineteenth Century.* Washington, D.C.: Smithsonian Institution Press, 1980.

New Jersey Pottery to 1840. Trenton: New Jersey State Museum, an Exhibition, March 18-May 12, 1972.

Ormsbee, Thomas H. *English China and Its Marks.* New York: Channel Press-Deerfield Editions, Ltd., 1959.

The Pottery & Porcelain of N.J. Prior to 1876. Newark, N.J.: The Newark Museum Association, Catalogue of Exhibition Feb. 1 to March 20, 1915.

The Pottery & Porcelains of N.J. 1688-1900. Newark, N.J.: Newark Museum, An Exhibition April 8-May 11, 1947.

Ramsey, John. *American Potters and Pottery.* Michigan: Ars Ceramica Ltd., 1976.

Robinson, Dorothy and Bill Feeny. *The Official Price Guide to American Pottery & Porcelain.* Orlando, Florida: The House of Collectibles, 1980.

Spargo, John. *Early American Pottery and China.* New York: The Century Co. 1926. Reissued Charles E. Tuttle, Rutland, Vt., 1974.

_____, *The Potters and Potteries of Bennington.* Boston: Houghton Mifflin Co., 1926. Reissued Dover Publications, 1972.

Thayer, Theodore. *As We Were the story of Old Elizabethtown.* Elizabeth, New Jersey: The Grossmann Publishing Co., Inc., 1964. Published for the N.J. Historical Society.

Watkins, Lura W. *Early New England Potters and their Wares.* Cambridge, Massachusetts: Harvard University Press, 1950. Reprinted by Archon Books, 1968.

Webster, D.B. *The Brantford Pottery.* R.O.M., 1968.

White, Margaret E. *The Decorative Arts of Early New Jersey.* N.J. Historical Series, 25. Princeton: Van Nostrand Company, Inc., 1964.

Winton, Andrew L. and Kate Barber. *Norwalk Potteries.* Canaan, New Hampshire: Phoenix Publishing for Friends of Lockwood House, Inc., 1981.

Bulletin of The American Ceramic Society. "William Bloor", 6 (1): 1937, 23-31.
_____, 20 (1): 1941. Reprint. 25-27.
Cincinnati City Directories. 1849-70, 1873-85. Cincinnati Historical Society.
Chandler, L. Reginald. "The Methods of Early American Potters." *Antiques,* April 1924, 174-8.
Cox, Lucille. "Isaac Watts Knowles." *American Ceramic Society Bulletin,* 21 (8), August 15, 1942, 152-7.
_____, "The Story of John Goodwin, Pioneer Potter." *The Bulletin of the American Ceramic Society,* 21 (11) Nov. 15, 1942, 241-7.
East Liverpool Review. May 1942, April 1960.
Godden, Geoffrey, Letter to Author, 17 January, 1985.
Knittle, Rhea Mansfield. "Muskingum County, Ohio, Pottery." *Antiques,* July 1924, 15-18.
Mountford, A.R., Letter to Author, 4 January, 1985.
Potters Herald. 1 April 1937, 15 July 1937, 12 August 1937.
Remensnyder, John P. "The Potters of Poughkeepise," Antiques, July 1966, 90-96.
Smith, John., Letter to Author, 24 December, 1984.
Stradling, J. G. "American Ceramics and The Philadelphia Centennial." *The Magazine Antiques,* July, 1976.
Trenton City Directories. 1865-9, 1877.
Vodrey, William. Letter, East Liverpool Museum of Ceramics Archives, Ohio.
Watkins, Lura Woodside. "Henderson of Jersey City & His Pitchers." *Antiques L,* Dec. 1946, 388-392.
Year Book. Dutchess County Historical Society 25, 1940, 73-77.

INDEX

The terms yellow ware and rockingham are not addressed to any degree in this index since they are listed on almost every page.
All index references to illustrations will be written in italics form.